Gabriela Ciucurovschi

7 Steps For Children's Happiness

Principles That Will Help Your Children For A Lifetime

Descrierea CIP a Bibliotecii Naționale a României
CIUCUROVSCHI, GABRIELA
7 Steps For Children's Happiness
- Principles That Will Help Your Children For A
Lifetime / Gabriela Ciucurovschi ;
trad.: Ana-Maria Briana Belciug.
- București : Benefica International, 2012
ISBN 978-606-93343-1-7

I. Belciug, Ana-Maria-Briana (trad.)
159.922.7

Author: Gabriela Ciucurovschi
Translator: Briana Belciug
Copyediting: Bessie Gantt
Cover Design: Anatoli Ciucurovschi
Cover Illustration: Shutterstock / Yaviki

You can read this book in English, French, Spanish, Italian,
German, Portuguese, Romanian

BENEFICA INTERNATIONAL

*To my son Aleksei,
without whom I would not have had
all this knowledge,
with gratitude and love.*

Look through this book and if the information within resonates for you, if you feel it can help you, read it! If not, search somewhere else because, most probably, your soul has other needs at the moment.

Gabriela Ciucurovschi

Contents

FOREWORD 7

1. A GOOD MODEL TO FOLLOW! 13

2. A UNIQUE BEING 25

3. HABITS, OUR SECOND NATURE 35

Our Everyday Food 43
Thoughts – A Different Kind of Food 47
Choices 56

4. DISCIPLINE 61

5. INGREDIENTS OF A HAPPY LIFE 75

Forgiveness 75
Unconditional Love 83
Prayer 88
Values 93

6. MORAL LAWS WE CANNOT
TRANSGRESS 111

Fear 111
Anger 120
Guilt 125
Envy and Hatred 128
Pride 130
Critical Judgment 131

ABOUT "SINS" AND THEIR CONSEQUENCES 135

7. PARENTING 137

FOLLOW YOUR INTUITION 137
A LIFETIME EXPERIENCE 138
A PARENT'S SACRIFICE 140
GENERATION GAP 142
GENERATION CONNECTION 144
LEGACY GIVEN FORTH 148

ACKNOWLEDGMENTS 151

Foreword

*Every man bears his childhood
as an overturned bucket over his head…
its contents trickle upon us throughout our lifetime
no matter how often we may change our clothes…*

Heimito von Doderer

Every parent wants the best for his or her child. From that wish to its materialization in your child's life you have a long way to go to get to the place where your actions actually contribute to the achievement of this wish.

At the beginning of your relationship with your child there is a positive intention. A positive intention has a value in and of itself, but when it comes to your own child you are very interested in the final result. What exactly is this "good" you want for your child? Does what you do really contribute to his best interest? How does "the good" look from your child's point of view?

There are many wishes we all have for our children. Unfortunately, we do not always realize in time that under the avalanche of things we want for our child there is an essential one: his happiness. In general, you think you want him to be healthy, to get good grades, to be obedient; you want him to become somebody, to get a job or another, etc.

A happy man is an accomplished man. He is a man who enjoys life as it is, with all its ups and downs.

However, our key to happiness resides in childhood. Our ability to be happy and satisfied exists in the things accumulated during that period of time, especially in the first years of life. The values we accumulate back then represent the foundation of our lives. The mark that the parents put on their children through the education they give them, through the values they transmit to them, through the bonded connection they create with them is very important for the future grown-ups.

Every child wants to be loved and to have his parents' appreciation and approval. No matter the age, even if he is twenty or fifty years old, the relationship of a child with his parents and what they have seeded in his soul will accompany him all his life. It influences him on the deepest level of his inner life, and it acts in invisible ways upon his whole existence.

From the other perspective of the parent-child relationship, of the child's role in our life as parents, I will utter only this statement: he or she is the mirror of our becoming. It is the superior joy of raising a soul through our love and wisdom; and for a child to become a beautiful and mature fruit, the roots themselves need to be beautiful and mature.

My study of psychology, my own experience as a mother, and my fascination with human nature made me realize, many years ago, the impact of the relationship between parent and child at a conscious level but especially at an unconscious one. In other words, the importance of what message the parent sends his or her child in a subliminal way through attitude, behavior, and, last but not least, through thoughts.

This book can help you become aware of the impact you have as a parent on the evolution and growth of your child, but also on her happiness. It helps you push aside layers of conditioning and allows you to perceive things in their essence and simplicity. Most of them are things you know, you feel, but that you forget to take into account during this race of life when you tend to lose your priorities.

It is possible you do not see a great advantage in this awareness. Still, once you become aware of something, things change around you. Your reactions will not be the same because now you understand their consequences and see that you may not want these consequences to come to pass. You do not have to think now that the whole future of your child depends only on you. Everything you offer her as a parent passes through the filter of her personality. And this filter does not depend on you anymore. What depends on you is the raw material. Your duty is to make sure that this raw material, processed by your child's personality, will be healthy and beautiful. Do not be worried about feeling that you are not perfect. Nobody is perfect. But there is always a way to do things better.

Being a parent is not the easiest job. Many parents would like to know more things at the beginning of this process of raising and educating a child. One can learn the job of parenting mostly by seeing and doing things. The parent grows up the same time as his child. Parents and children, we evolve together. What really matters is the direction.

In order not to lose the right direction, you need to see things as a whole and understand those mechanisms and universally valid laws that act in every person's life that may be out of your control.

Acknowledging them, you will be able to be the good parent *you* want to be and to support your child during his evolution so that he becomes what *he* wants to be.

The experience of every life is unique. However, there is a common denominator, and this denominator can help us understand the inner human urges that are universal to all people. Each and every person you see has a background history sprinkled with miseries and joys, with fears and frustrations, with desires and needs. In the center of each of these histories is the relationship with that person's mother and father. Everything stars from here.

1

A Good Model to Follow!

*When the fathers eat sour grapes,
the children's teeth are set on edge.*
– Proverb

No matter how many things you would *say* to your child in an effort to give him a good education, nothing is of higher value than your behavior. What you *do* regarding your child—and other people too—the attitude you show, the way you take action in life—these are his real standards. It is useless to tell your child, "It is not nice to lie," if he hears you telling your workmate that you are sick and you cannot come to work because you are going to spend a day with your family or even go visit your parents' farm to help them with their harvest, for example.

You are your child's model!

For you, considering the context, the "little white lie" does not have the value of a "real" lie because you know you are going to do something special or to help your elderly parents, and you don't mind using some mild subterfuge to spend valuable time with your family or to make your parents' lives easier.

Of course, as an adult you will inevitably tell little untruths because there are many life situations when you cannot simply blurt out the truth. Either you have to stretch the truth just a little bit in order not to offend or hurt somebody or you cannot tell truth for any number of justifiable reasons. For your boss, your parents' farm is not important, and he or she would not agree to let you miss work for two days if things are busy at work. What should you do? You cannot get sick at somebody's order. And then, if you really got sick you would not be able to work at the farm and help your parents anyway.

Today your child hears you telling a lie at work, and tomorrow he hears you telling his grandmother, "No, Mother, I did not give him French fries," after he has just finished eating them. At one point, the child begins to think that it is easier to lie than tell the truth. Why should he give so many explanations for what he wants when instead he can simply say what his parents want to hear and then mind his own business?

Be aware every moment of the impact of your actions upon your child!

I have met people for whom the lie was more convenient than the truth. They used to lie without thinking too much about it, without even blinking. It simply became their common way of being.

I have always been fascinated by their ability. They take their actions so lightly without thinking too much about the consequences, about what it could happen if the truth came out. And even if they realize people do not believe them, they still cannot quit. For them it is easier this way: to close their eyes and to believe their own stories. However, I'm not just talking about pathological liars. Feeling more at ease either telling the truth or telling a lie, whether little white lies or big lies, represents one of the most important facets of our social lives as well as of our inner lives.

The ability to tell the truth depends on the ability to show yourself to the world as you are and to what extent you feel accepted by the world. And that acceptance is a felling that has its foundation in your early childhood that goes on to accompany you permanently in your relationships with others.

In general, people lie so that they get away from difficult situations that cause them conflict or to improve their image in the eyes of the others. Why do they feel the need to improve their image? Because what they think about *themselves* does is not at a level where they consider they can be accepted and appreciated by others.

Here we have reached an important issue: many times the child invents different scenarios or lies about themselves in order to be accepted by adults. But, if you, as the child's parent, shows him how much you love her just as she is with all her sensitivities, her fears, her weakness, she would not have to present herself in a different way in front of you.

There are many situations when parents say one thing to their child and yet do the opposite. They try very hard to offer their child good lessons on the right way to act, but they consider that in their case the rules they are preaching do not always apply.

Do not say one thing
and do another!

The real lesson is made and taught through facts and action. The words you say only have value if they are attended by facts to reinforce them. Thus, what you say has no value for the child if what you do does not sustain what you transmit verbally.

More than that, your child will be adrift and will reject your teachings if they are not exemplified and supported by your behavior. And instead of obtaining the deliverable lesson you desire in your child, you will get negative feedback. The behavior of saying one thing and doing another creates in your child discomfort and inner conflict. Following this conflict, the child has to make a choice. There is a bigger chance that his choice will be what is fortified by your behavior and not to what you tell him.

If you are a disorderly person but you tell your child to gather his toys because "he must learn how to be tidy because tidiness is important," the first time he is able to act on his own choice, he will reject being tidy. Why shouldn't sloppiness work for him the way it works for you, which requires much less effort than picking up his toys.

You do not know in how this inner conflict may affect your child. He may think to himself, "Is my mother lying?" And you do not know how he will answer this question. And if he reaches the conclusion that Mother is lying, you cannot imagine how big the inner discomfort caused by this issue may be. It may be possible that he draw a general conclusion that what you tell him it is not believable. And this is how such a small grain of distrust can forever damage a relationship almost from its very beginning.

Be aware of the conflicts you raise within your child's soul!

What you transmit to your child through your personality has a great impact on his future personality and his nature.

If you are an anxious person, you will behave accordingly and will create the premise of this expression within your child as well. If you are a reserved and incommunicative person, realize that this is what you transmit to your child. You are her model.

If you are a person who does not lose patience easily and who is not afraid when a difficult situation occurs, if you express a trustful attitude toward yourself and to your ability of finding a solution, the child will notice and internalize it, and the probability that she later will manifest the same attitude toward challenges is very high.

We are not absolute duplicates of our parents, but an important part of what we are is due to them and our interaction with them. If you have a habit of lying all the time, do not expect your son or daughter to tell the truth.

If you are a person with many vices, think what an impact these vices have upon your child. See if you can come to terms with the idea that later he will most likely have the same habits as you. What would you feel as a parent when you see your child staying up late at night? Would you worry that he was not getting enough rest?

That his natural sleeping pattern was suffering from getting the nights and days switched around? To you, an adult, it may seem natural to stay awake at nights; you always have an important reason to do so as you always find explanations when it comes to your actions. Well, you should know you are not the only person who does this. Everybody does it.

When you create a precedent, you cannot control what follows from it. And usually what follows exceeds the precedent in its extent. If today you give somebody a finger, the next day the person will ask for your whole hand. If you prove yourself sympathetic with regard to a co-worker's problems and you did not put him on the list of absentees from work a few times when he was not in fact there, in a very high percentage of these cases, the situation will repeat itself again. But it will be repeated in a way that will greatly exceed the initial situation. Most probably he will miss work more and more or he will be late for work more often, claiming that you should understand him every time.

If your lifestyle was characterized by staying up late at night and, more than that, you made a habit of letting your child to stay up with you, why are you surprised that once he becomes a teenager he goes to bed toward morning and wakes up long after lunch? As I said, a precedent is an action that instigates other actions over which you have no control— or to put things back on track the way you want, a radical action is required.

In the case of your children's education, these issues are much more delicate. This happens for one single reason: your relationship with your child changes constantly. It is not like the relationship with a colleague or your boss, which stays mostly the same, becoming only friendlier or more tense. Your child's state of mind is in continuous flux. Now he is a baby, tomorrow or the day after tomorrow he will be a little student, then an awkward tweener, a teenager and, suddenly, you see him becoming an adult. From a certain moment to another you must respond differently to him because his capacity for understanding the world and the place he is coming from emotionally and intellectually changes.

A precedent, once it is created, attracts situations that exceed the limits of the previous precedent. If several times, for example, in a matter of relatively little importance, you prove to your child a total confidence in his own decision making, he will be able to permanently extend this confidence toward even more important situations, and he will become more and more confident in the decisions he makes.

If a parent shows a disrespectful attitude toward his or her child, meaning that the parent does not take into account what the child wants and the parent's adult interests are a priority in most cases, that person may complain in years to come that his own child ignores him. And this after the parent raised him with such an effort! We often hear parents voice the expression, "Why do you raise children? So that they do not show you respect when they grow up?" Well, after you made it imperative for him all his childhood to do different things without your teaching him the purpose behind them, only for the reason that "he has to," after you imposed your adult point of view every time without listening what he had to say, are you surprised now that your own child is disrespectful to you?

If you want to have a respectful child, start showing her respect from an early age. Show her that what she wants, what she feels, and her point of view matter to you. Show her this in all your actions.

> **Show your child that what she wants, what she feels, and her point of view matter to you.**

Do you want to have a child who can manage through life? Show him that you manage yourself successfully through difficult situations. Show him you are the master of your life and that you do not wait for other people to solve your problems.

Do you want to have a joyful child? Show him that you know how to laugh. Show him that you know how to enjoy life. Laugh with him.

The models around him represent an important aspect for the education of the child. The child learns by seeing how the people around him react in different situations and by noticing which the esteemed behaviors are. There are three main sources of role models: the family, school, and the child's group of friends. In order for his personality to evolve beautifully, the child needs good models to follow, people who inspire him and help him discover his inner self.

Your child needs
positive role models.

If we look toward the past, every one of us can tell to what extent teacher X influenced us, who held our attention by telling beautiful stories and by his or her humor, or teacher Y who was very severe and whose class nobody could afford to miss. If the teacher X made you appreciate people who tell beautiful stories and taught you how to tell a story, teacher Y inspired you through fear and made you understand that there are people you should not mess with.

If you roll back the film of your childhood, you also remember your father's friend who made everybody burst in laughter every time with his jokes. Everyone had a great time when he was around, and that was why he was often invited to your house. You were all ears when that friend talked. You liked the relaxed atmosphere and the general joy. Then you were able to develop a sense of humor yourself, and you enjoyed when your friends laughed at your jokes.

The recipe for developing a personality is complex. The personality is created after mixing a few ingredients: the inner structure of a person, the sensitivity, the natural talents, the environment, etc. In the end, the combination of those inherent traits and the parents' essential role in the developing process of the child's personality is magic.

The personality is the complex result of combining and transforming many factors.

People withstand many influences during their lifetime. They gather, on the way of their becoming, something from every person they connect with. On the way of your child's becoming, what he takes from you represents the keystone for all the subsequent influences and transformations. The little child is a mirror of his or her parents. The child reflects their beliefs, behaviors, and influences; the environment they provide; and the atmosphere they create in their home. If you want your reflection to be bright, first of all take care of yourself. Take care of yourself in relation to your child and also in relation to the world. Whether you like it or not, you are a role model for your child. But what kind of model are you? This is only for you to decide and act on accordingly.

2

A Unique Being

Know thyself.
– Written on the frontispiece of the Delphi temple

No matter how much he looks like his mother, like his father, or his grandparents, your child is unique. He is a distinct individual from all the others. No matter how much he looks like other children of his age or how much he has in common with them, there are differences, and you, as a parent, feel this thing the best.

Actually, every person is unique, and even if on the outside your child's behavior looks like the other people's behaviors, on the inside there are differences regarding the quality and the quantity. Personalities can resemble each other, they can have a lot of things in common, but this does not mean that they are identical.

Every child is unique, and he has to be treated as such.

This difference and uniqueness of ours is a wonderful thing. This constitutes the spice of all of our social relationships. If we were all the same, we would get bored of each other quickly. And meeting other people would not bring nearly as much joy.

This difference helps us come up with different solutions for the same problem, to contribute in different ways to our circle of friends and to our conversations, to think and act in a unique way. But also due to this uniqueness, people perceive things differently.

Our unique perception of things influences all of our personal goings-on. Thanks to our individually unique ways of seeing things, people can understand things completely differently from one another when it comes to the same event. People may even see things that do not exist. Every person has his or her own truth. For any one event or issue there can be countless perspectives, and each one of them can be real.

What does it mean for you as a parent knowing the uniqueness of your child? It means the joy of really knowing your child. It means knowing who she is beyond the social conventions. For the child it means the possibility of expressing herself, of sharing what she really is. We all hold inside of ourselves the need to be understood and accepted. It means comfort for your child because she does not need to conceal anything; she does not need to be another person. It means the certitude that she is accepted and loved just the way she is. It is important to understand this uniqueness of every one of us. Even if it seems a simple thing and that it stands to reason, the majority of people behave as if they really do not understand it.

Parents tend to compare their children with other children of their age, with their brothers and sisters or with themselves at that age. It is frustrating for the child to be compared to another person. For her this equals not being understood and being considered inferior to the person she is compared to. It is a slippery slope from here to the birth of self-distrust.

Comparisons fill our lives, yet they do nothing but bring with them bitterness and distrust. The child looks at her peers and craves a better computer, more expensive clothes, and the unlimited freedom her friend has that she does not.

The comparisons make us look in our neighbor's yard and cherish what he has. We often forget to cherish what we have.

The social life and the education that we get at school, outside of our lessons from home, teaches us that only those who throw themselves into competition and who win are valuable people. Big error!

Every person has value, and she does not have to prove her value to anyone.

**Every person has value,
and she does not have to prove
her value to anyone.**

This rabid spirit of competition can give birth to a lot of monsters: envy, selfishness, lack of tolerance. When, actually, the only competition we should enter is the one with ourselves. This competition should be the only one to interest us. I do not think that geniuses and those who've brought big benefits to mankind were in competition with others. Whom should they compete with if their abilities and knowledge were obviously superior to the others? They just felt that they could do more.

The only competition we should enter is the one with ourselves.

Every one of us has a potential to succeed, and I think this is a purpose itself. People have assimilated this spirit of competition so much that many times they wake up in a competition within their couple relationship as well. Very often this relationship becomes a fight for power. If you roll the film back to many years earlier, you will see you were thrown into this competition when you were very little. You probably already know how much this competition can ruin the couple relationship. The couple relationship, like other relationships too, should be a communion, not a competition.

Saturated by models, by social rules that push us toward standardization, we risk who we really are. The road to yourself is paved with experiences and choices but also with a growth of your own conscience. Sometimes it is hard to choose to be yourself and not simply follow the mold others have set. Oftentimes it is hard to realize who you really are. Some people need a lifetime to find out.

Help your child discover himself. Not everybody is Einstein, but everybody has something valuable within him. All he needs to do is to discover what it is. This value does not reduce itself only to a talent, a vocation toward one field or another, such as music, painting, mathematics, etc. It may be a personality feature—such as kindness, honesty, joyfulness, etc.—springing from his human nature. No matter the nature of this value, discovered in time it may grow and reach maturity by its own expression and manifestation.

I know a person in the presence of whom all your sadness disappears. You forget about your troubles, and all of a sudden you feel better because he sends out beams of joy and kindness. Embellishing the life of the people around you and turning it into a more beautiful one is a big gift. You can be a valuable person because you always jump to help your neighbor when he needs it; you can be a valuable person for the good taste and the way you decorate your house, for the talent of telling stories that everybody around you gathers to listen to, for the garden you take care of and for the flowers you grow with love, for the harmonious family you have—to your credit!—for your serenity, etc.

Saturated by models, by social rules that push us toward standardization, we risk forgetting who we really are.

As a parent, you want to keep your child safe. You want to know he is on a certain trajectory.

You want to know he studies well, he has a good job, and he is starting a loving family. It is possible that all these things do not make him happy. It is possible that inside of him there is a struggle between what he really wants to be and what he is. Be aware of his wishes. Be aware of what he is. He is a unique person. You just have to pay attention and to notice. Encourage him to discover himself. The child needs your support throughout this process. Certainly it is not easy for you. And sometimes it can be painful. But in the end, the result is worth it. Life rewards us for all our well-done work.

Personality formation is a long-term process. It begins in childhood, it is strongly defined in the adolescence, but it continues to evolve at an adult age too, when it undergoes deep transformations. Personality formation is accomplished after many experiences and choices have been made, after assimilating models of social behavior, but also after discovering oneself.

Your role as a parent in this process is delicate, important, and it is not without difficulty. The difficulty results from the two facets of this role: on one side, you direct your child toward the assimilation of behavior models necessary for living in a society, and on the other side, you help him to discover himself and to behave like an individual.

The support you offer your child so that he discovers his own personality will save him later from many frustrations. Parents are happy when the child resembles them, and this is healthy as long as what he takes over from them is a positive thing for his life. However, he needs to discover himself, to discover the things that define him and not his parents. This discovery, understanding, and manifestation of his inner self will make him feel good in his own skin. He needs to understand who he is and to define himself independently of his mother and father. He does not have to be a copy of anyone. He must be himself.

You, as a parent, help him during this process where you have to delicately follow the manifestation of his inner self and the integration of himself into social situations.

You will probably ask yourself right now: how can I know what and who his inner self is? Well, his inner self is expressed by all those things that he enjoys and that make him feel good. If you pay attention, you will notice them. You just have to let him express them as far as they do not harm anyone else. Do not burden your child with the fulfilling of *your* dreams because he is a totally different person who will have his own dreams.

Do not burden your child with the fulfilling of your dreams because he is a totally different person who will have his own dreams.

Do not put on your child's shoulders your frustrations and your failures. Do not think, "If I was not able to do it, at least my child should do this," because you do not know if what you wanted for yourself is right for him. Let him discover what he wants.

Every personality and individuality represents a universe to explore—by himself and by others. The more we discover parts of the uniqueness of the person next to us, the more we understand him and the more we approach the essence of his being. Basically, we all want to surpass the barrier of the studied behaviors. We all need sincere expressions that spring from the depth of the other being. The benefits of expressing the self are great. The interpersonal relationships will be warmer, closer, and more natural. I think this is how you want to be the relationship with your child, too.

3

Habits, Our Second Nature

Try to begin everything you do well from the start
because the progress of a process depends
on what you put down at the beginning.
— Omraam Mikhael Aivanhov

During all our lives as grown-ups we struggle with our habits. As children we do not become aware of their importance, and when we realize how much they affect us, we also begin to understand how hard it is to change them.

It is said that habits are like our second nature. No description could be more fitting. If we think just for a moment on all of our habits we show during one day, we realize that most of our lives is based on habits.

Our lives are based on habits.

The habit of drinking coffee in the morning, of waking up late, the habit of leaving home late or, on the contrary, of reaching a place on time, the habit of eating at a certain time of day, the habit of calling Mother in the evening, the habit of talking a little bit about a particular colleague, the habit of humming a song while driving, the habit of going to bed late, the habit of smiling, the habit of arranging your hair a certain way, of throwing your clothes everywhere, etc. And the list for each of us is long. It is very long.

Our daily repeated actions are so many that every day seems to be the same. Many times, the difference is made by a meeting with your friends, a show, an evening spent reading, a nice moment with the family. Otherwise, the days run one after the other, having as a base the same actions over and over again on our part.

But habits have their role. They make us feel safe because they offer us an experience whose consequences we already know. They offer us the pleasure of the ritual, such as the ritual of having coffee every morning with your husband or wife and of enjoying the quiet silence of the morning or of the whole family gathering every evening for dinner.

As a child, for example, the habit of coming home from school and telling your family what happened over the day satisfies your need to share the things from your life with the people close to you, the need to be understood or to be supported and advised when you are not sure about the meaning of the events. Becoming a grown-up, this habit can help you in the communication with your new family, benefitting from its support and empathy in the progress of the events from your life, and it can reinforce the couple relationship as well as the relationship with your child. Many children suffer from the lack of communication with their parents, and this happens not because the parents do not love them, but because they did not learn how to communicate.

Habits offer us safety.

Habits are not only, in most cases, permanent, they are also of great importance. They reflect upon us, and they can do us much good or do quite the opposite.

There are two important aspects of this issue: 1) we get accustomed to most of these habits during our childhood and 2) they are difficult to change.

We get accustomed to many habits during childhood, and they are difficult to change.

This is why parents must be careful regarding the habits their child is creating. And even more, parents must contribute so that they acquire good habits. Good habits make our life better and brighter, easier and more comfortable, while bad habits can lead to conflict and drama.

Habits influence the quality of our lives.

You can get sick or become overweight as a result of an extremely unhealthy diet and, from here, the discomfort, the lower self-esteem, the isolation, the lack of self-confidence—the combination of all of these—can, in the end, make you feel squeezed and without vitality. On the other hand, if you are a person who makes a habit of eating lightly in the evening and at a certain time, you can be sure that one of the reasons that you rest well every night is the fact that you do not have a full stomach at bedtime.

Let us consider another situation that does not have to do with food. Have you heard the expression "mad at life?" There are people so used to seeing only the ugly things in their life or only the things they do not have that they completely ignore what they *do* have. And in this way they come to live day after day mad at life not realizing what they are missing and ignoring the beautiful things in their life. And more than that, they lose with every unoffered smile, with every good gesture they did not do for the others, with every unthought beautiful thought, the chance of making a better life for themselves. It is their chance, and they lose it by ignoring it. These are some examples of the effects that bad habits can have upon somebody's life.

But let us see also what a good habit can do. Let us just imagine how your child made a habit of being an indulgent person. This will be of a great importance in her life, helping combat sadness, anger, and other negative states of mind by accepting others just the way they are. This positive mindset will reflect upon her good inner being and the peace and harmony she will experience. Not being a person who criticizes and judges others at every turn will cause other people to feel good around her.

And also, how many ugly things can happen when you are angry? When you are angry, you can say things to hurt the loved person; you can even say untruthful things, only out of the need to let the anger out. And the harsh words can remain in our mind and heart for a long period of time, affecting and influencing our actions.

Certainly, the indulgence has its limits. If you are too tolerant, you can be easily "used" by others. That is why it is good to help your child understand that tolerance has its limits, too. It is valuable when we accept others the way they are and we do not judge them in comparison to what we want them to be.

Habits can make our life difficult or they can improve it.

Our habits represent us. They shape our character. They define our personality. You can see how a person is after the habits she has.

If we meet a person who sleeps in general ten to twelve hours a day, and then she needs two more hours to wake up, it is a great probability that she is not a very efficient person in what she does. And what has to be done during the day she is not able to accomplish easily. When engines are asleep for such a long time, it is difficult to make them function all of a sudden at their high capacity.

There are people who you need to avoid when they get up because they are glum, they have aggressive attitudes toward others, and they just want to be left alone. This permanent reaction in the moment of waking up has become a habit for them. And we cannot think, "Why is X so upset every time she wakes up?" without upsetting the person's present reality.

We can realize that something from that person's past created this habit. Formerly, at some point, there was a real reason why that person was upset at the time of waking up. In time, this reaction was fixed, and yet this mannerism became a habit without having any causality in the immediate reality.

Habits, habits... If you are a person who is always late to meetings, it can be said that you do not have much respect for the others at the meeting. If you are a person who complains all the time, and you transform every meeting with others into an unpleasant experience, burdening them with your problems, people will begin to try to avoid you; you will become a presence that most of your friends will not want. Your friends will think that it is easier for you to complain than for you to do something real in order to sincerely try to change whatever the negative situation may be.

Most of our habits come from our childhood, and they affect our entire life.

Habits manifest themselves in absolutely all aspects of our lives. However, there are a few categories of more important habits that crucially influence our life, both in the short and long term.

Our Everyday Food

Some of the most deeply rooted habits that we try to change are our dietary habits. Nobody revises their dietary routines because they discovered better tastes—only because the person sees this aspect from another perspective.

There comes a moment when we realize that health is important. During your childhood you heard this many times, but you do not pay attention as a child. You have your whole life before you. What do you care? When, finally, you realize its importance, you notice you have to change a lot of dietary habits. And you start a terrific fight, and you make effort over effort to change such a small routine, for example, not to eat after a certain time of the day or to avoid certain categories of foods. And you succeed in keeping this new habit for a period of time; you are very proud for this. Then, you do not know how, something happens and you return to the old habits. After you deprived yourself for a period of time of something that you enjoyed before, after you gathered all your forces to fight against something stronger than you and you succeeded in winning, later, with all the gained success, the old habit reveals its presence. Why? And how does this happen after so much effort?

Somewhere, deep inside us, habits became our second nature, and people make efforts to change them only when the situations are dire. There are few people who succeed in doing this thing for good, freely and unconstrained.

Habits are difficult to change.

Many people return to their old habits, even if the effort they make to change them is huge. And then, the disappointment and the self-distrust is even higher than before.

With respect to food there are many theories, sometimes so many and so different that at some point you do not know anymore which one to follow. In this avalanche of information and commercials that surround us, we must find our ability to see the things in their simplicity. No matter how much information would flood us, there are a few simple nutrition principles that can be transmitted to our children. But this involves the parent's personal example and a conscious control of the food we buy and that is in the house within reach of the children.

The action of eating is one of the most frequent behaviors in everyone's life. We eat at home, at work, we have a snack on the road, and the fact is that for the most of us this activity ends up occupying quite some time as a whole. Without realizing it, we consume impressive quantities of food.

Eating is one of man's greatest pleasures, and one of his greatest addictions. We depend on tastes, flavors, shapes, and the nice culinary experiences that we've experienced before. And the fact that eating takes so much time from our life also shows how great the effect of this habit is on us. The consequences are enormous. The person who fasts at least once month feels the strong but also subtle influence of the food not only upon the body, but especially upon our psyche.

Children adopt many dietary habits from grown-ups.

People eat all sorts of unhealthy food from a lack of knowledge, healthy choices, or from bad habits. From all these, I think the last two go hand in hand, and they are the strongest. In a way or another, every one of us knows when he/she does something wrong. Only we do not pay always pay too much attention to that sense.

Children adopt many dietary habits from the grown-ups around them, the habit of eating a healthy breakfast, of drinking sodas or not, of eating certain types of food, home cooked or fast food, of eating too late in the evening, etc.

A healthy diet is the key to a healthy body, and our happiness depends so much on our health. In a very strange way, almost paradoxically, most grown-ups value health, but they do not act accordingly until they are in danger of losing their health. Unhealthy habits will later determine the health of your child when he is a grown-up. He will have to work hard to get rid of these habits. In order to lose weight, to improve his health or only to keep it, he will be aware that he must set some rules and respect them. The good habits that you transmit to your child will save him the future effort of having to do and undo, of having to start all over again, and it will help him focus his energy toward other constructive things in his life.

Thoughts – A Different Kind of Food

– We draw energy from our thoughts –

Few things are so present in our life as the thoughts we have. Our thoughts permanently accompany us, even whether we eat or not, sleep or not. They flow into an internal stream from where we permanently withdraw our energy. If our thoughts are beautiful, optimistic, confident, and tolerant, then the energy we feel is a beneficial one. And you realize it is beneficial judging after the well being that accompanies it. If your thoughts accompany fear, envy, sadness, etc., then goodbye, well being. You will feel either a lack of energy or the energy you already have will tend to ruin everything good in your life. We all call it negative energy. Have you ever seen a rolled-up carpet? Imagine that in the center of this roll are your thoughts. When you lay out the carpet, you will show the path of your life. The moment your thoughts come into being, the premises for their materialization are created, too.

Our thoughts are as important as our actions. There is energy in each one of them. This energy will attract to your life the things you are thinking of, no matter if you want them or not. You are thinking of them, and this is enough. Thinking has its own mechanisms. The way we think has at its basis some settings, some conditionings, that come from childhood. It works like a filter: to a certain level of our conscience we do not see the reality as it is but as we are used to seeing it.

Let us say that a person from our group of friends says a certain thing that hurts you. You feel this situation annoys you, and at the same time, you feel the anger growing inside you. Finally, you conclude he did it on purpose. He intentionally wanted to hurt you. This is because he had to settle accounts with you, because one time you said something that bothered him, too. Yeah, you even remember how hard he took whatever it was that you said. You could clearly see it on his face at the time. And you continue thinking these thoughts until the conclusion is undeniable. You cannot be wrong. That is it! X did it certainly to hurt you. Otherwise, why would you feel so bad?

Then, during a subsequent discussion with that person you find out that, actually, what he had done had nothing to do with you but with somebody else. And you are amazed to realize the entire thinking mechanism was misleading. You watch with astonishment, you replay in your mind the film of the whole situation; you also reroll the film of your brain and you ask yourself in a stupor: how was that possible?

Well, here is an interpretation that does not represent anything new. When you were little, your elder sister teased you all the time. She did so because she felt better this way; she felt strong and important. But you thought she was doing it to mock you. She was doing it to hurt you. Actually, her behavior had nothing to do with you but with her. But how could you know that?

Being frequently treated like that during your childhood, you became sensitive to people's observations. It is a sensitivity that becomes second nature to you. It often happens then that you think that people want to hurt you or put you in a bad light. And in this way you extended your childhood experience to your life experiences. Almost without even realizing it. You created a pattern for your thinking that would continue without deviating every time.

Our thinking works like a horse harnessed to a cart. It always knows how to arrive at home by itself. If you do not bridle and guide it, it will carry you every time to the same location. This location is a fixed target. This location is the belief we acquire in our childhood. Our thinking always follows the same route. The starting point is the belief—a deeply rooted conviction in our childhood that at most times we are not even aware of.

There is a natural tendency to prove to ourselves the things we believe in .

If I think that people have the tendency to mock me, my thinking will go along the route that proves to me that people are in fact mocking and disregarding me. If I think I am a person whose opinion matters, my thinking will go the route that will not raise barriers in my expressing my opinion but, on the contrary, will contribute to the affirmation of a clear and strong point of view. If I think that everything I've accomplished in my life it was done only with great effort and that I am predicted to accomplish things only with difficultly, only after I've struggled a lot, then my thinking will go along the route where I will not notice the easy ways of getting the things that I want, only the adversity.

Every person perceives life in the light of the attitude he has toward life, toward his value judgments, toward his convictions. His perception is the reality he lives in. It may happen that two people who go through the same experience together have completely different perceptions regarding what had happened.

At first you may think that one of them is lying. And yet, neither is lying. It is just that the perceived reality by each of them differs depending on the inner reality of each. It is not the objective reality that affects us but the subjective way that we refer to it. What influences our way of perceiving things is found in the beliefs acquired during our childhood and that constitute the basis of the entire scaffolding of our later thinking.

> **It is not the objective reality that affects us, but the subjective way that we refer to it.**

It sometimes happens to us that we watch with admiration different people who have a positive approach to things. We see them confronting a problem, and we say to ourselves, "God, if this had happened to me, I would have been paralyzed with fear. I would not have been able to do anything in his situation. Why can I not react like this, too? Why can I not be as calm as he in order to see the things more clearly?" At that moment, we realize that it is about a learned reaction, a habit that we appropriated at a certain moment on the path of our life.

Consequently, there are not problems that matter but our reactions to these problems.

Everyone has problems. What makes the difference is the way in which we react to them. And in this case, the way we think, the way we perceive things, has an essential role, the angle from which we view the problem. The same problem may seem insurmountable for a person, and for somebody else it may be only a situation that is solved like any other situation.

No matter how difficult the situation we are confronting, we can find solutions for them. Everything is about not leaving ourselves dominated by fear because fear paralyzes our thoughts, our actions, and our ability to see clearly. If we stay calm and secure in our belief that things can be solved, the solution will come.

**Every problem has its solution.
This is a belief you need to transmit
to your child.**

It is true that the solution you find may be a totally different solution than the one you want. But this is the real magic of solving problems. If we hold onto a certain solution that we strongly want and want things to be done only in a certain way, then it is certain that the probability of solving that problem and finding another solution is very small. But, if we prove ourselves flexible and open to receiving any possible solution, we will also discover that other solutions are possible for the way out of the respective situation.

Positive thinking means being open to all possible situations.

One time, I had an employee who would come to me and say, "Boss, we have a problem." No matter the scope of the problem, this was his invariable expression. And he would look at me as if nothing beyond this problem existed. After a few similar situations, I realized that it was a pattern of behavior. Any situation a little more difficult than normal appeared to him as a "problem." The first time I said, "Tell me, Andrew, what is the problem?" Even if, I admit, his grave concern and expression frightened me. He was so serious that I automatically thought, "God, what has happened?" In time, I realized it was not about serious problems but about small obstacles inherent to almost any activity of any significance.

Then, I started to be slightly amused: "Another problem, Andrew?!"

When we realize the impact of some things acquired during our childhood, such as our habits or attitude toward life, we tend, on one side, to panic, overwhelmed by the responsibility to our child, and on the other side, to feel frustrated. We think that if we had had an education like X, things would have been different for us, too. If Mother had known to teach us all these things we would not have gone to such a great trouble! And, certainly, we would have known to offer our child more valuable guidance. But now, what should we do? Where do we start?

Panic and frustration do not solve anything. It is never too late to openly talk to your child. No matter the age of your child, this talk brings great benefits in your life. A huge energy will be unchained, a beneficial energy that will work to your advantage.

It is never too late to stop, to look at your child's face (maybe he is already a grown-up) and to see what he is telling you. Does his face express contentment and joy or tension and fear? What can you do if the latter is what you notice? You can find out exactly what is has caused him to suffer, you can give him some advice (but be careful: make sure he wants this, that he is open to receive your advice, and that, first of all, you are keeping his interests at the forefront and not your peace of mind or self-interest), and, most of all, you can support him emotionally. You can always do something more. We all aspire to a perfect life, but life is just the way it is: with ups and downs.

Let us close those doors that do not lead anywhere and let us open those that lead to a better life!

Thinking, attitude, and feelings all go hand in hand. And they all start from a grain of belief. A grain planted a long time ago in our past. A grain that, as time went on, we may not recognize anymore but around which we have weaved the spider web of our entire life. Open your eyes wide to see the grain that you planted in your child's soul through words but especially through your actions. These actions are the true measure of what you pass along to your child.

Choices

You reap what you sow.
Proverb

The way we go through life is marked by the choices we make. Any choice may open a way for us or it may close it off; it may help us evolve or it may pull us down.

The choices we make are part of us and of our daily routine. They are pieces of us and our personality. The way we decide to do a thing or another has sneaked, in time, into our daily habits.

All choices are important. I could even say that the ones that seem relatively small are most important. When we have to make a major decision, we usually take more time to analyze it. And we weigh almost everything that can help us make the best decision for ourselves. We pass easily over the minor choices. And yet…they have an impact on our life every day.

Every moment of our life depends on a choice. We choose to watch TV or to read, to walk or to drive, to go out with friends or to stay home with the family, to eat at McDonald's or to cook something, to make a good joke or a malicious one, to be late to work every time or to arrive on time, to look for a job until we find one or to give up after the first three attempts…and the list may go on as long as we exist.

None of these choices is neutral. Every one of them influences our life in one way or another. What helps us here is being conscious of our choices. Any choice has a consequence, a result. No matter how much the people around us and society in general influence us, the problems we have are our choices. And through them we decide on our life.

Our choices are not neutral.

The way you, the parent, make choices represents a model for your child. This model, this pattern of behavior may sneak insidiously into your child's behavior. Besides the fact that you are a model for your child in everything you do, while she is small you have an important role in her choices. You are the one who guides her, you direct her, and you advise her on the choices she makes. By the choices we make we can create the opportunity for certain things to happen or not. We open or we shut the door for the events in our life.

Let us say that a person is in search of a job. At one point she sees a job advertisement in a newspaper at a famous company. If she is a pessimist person and has a lack of confidence in what life can offer her, that person may consider there is not a chance to get that job because it is too big a company and certainly that you need connections to get in there. Thus, she shuts this door all by herself. If she is a positive person, she may think that is better not to lose any chance and that she must try any card life offers. Now, I can tell you this example is real and the person did not let the opportunity escape. And I can also tell you that she got the job. This was only an example. But life puts us permanently in front of these kinds of situations. Most of them are common life situations.

Our choices are submitted to a natural law, universally valid, of the consequences for each of our actions, for each of our choices, either at a behavior level or only at a thinking level. This is commonly known as the cause-and-effect law, and it acts the same for everybody. As the proverb says, "You reap what you sow."

Every choice, every action of ours has a consequence.

We see and feel this simple concept permanently on our own skin. What deserves to be remembered in the context of our subject is the fact that most of these casual grains are seeded during the childhood. The life we live is the effect, the consequence of our thoughts and actions resulting from the beliefs, the values, and the thinking settings acquired during our childhood.

I have witnessed situations where parents advised their children, still in the period of their formation, to exploit a situation to their advantage, even of this meant the violation of the other people's rights and interests. Everything seems okay apparently. "I am only acting in the interest of my child," they say. And, yet, how much harm can this principle cause in time to your child and the choice of acting on it? Acting only in virtue of your own interest will trigger the presence of many situations that, actually, your child does not want in her life. But, sometimes, the distance between cause and effect can be so large that she may not even realize where all this started from.

Being conscious of what you do and what you think, what you decide in your life, is a big responsibility to have on your shoulders.

It is easier to say that fate is responsible than to think how you could act in a different way in order to create a different result. Maybe we cannot explain everything that happens in our life. But most things, if we look carefully, connect with what we did or what we thought at some point.

Help your child discover this responsibility, and you will not regret it. This will make her be careful and not be indifferent to the choices she makes. Help her see life as a whole. Help her see things in a long-term perspective. Sometimes, what may be painful in the short term may bring many long-term benefits.

4

Discipline

*There is no luck
except where there is discipline.
— Irish proverb*

Both grown-ups and children love the freedom to do what we want. And, yet, without the existence of certain rules we will not be able to leave together in the world. Rules can make our life easier in society if we understand them, we accept them, and we internalize them. In terms of respecting society and its rules, I have only one amendment: first of all, pass any rule through the filter of your thinking and feeling.

There are also a lot of absurdities in addition to the rules meant to make our life easier. Do not burden yourself or your child with useless rules that do not bring you anything good.

For example, do not force your child into doing certain things in order to please the grown-ups if he does not want to do it—such as reciting the poem he learned at kindergarten in front of your guests only to prove his good education. Of course, it is nice to see children accumulating information and expressing it in a personal way. Yet, it is not good for the child to be forced into doing something just to please somebody else.

Pass every rule through your own thinking and feeling.

Discipline means the habit of respecting certain rules, the habit of having a program, of making a plan, and of acting accordingly in order to accomplish certain established purposes. For example, if you are to take an exam and you do not prepare or study, it is not probable that you will pass that exam. In order to be able to do well on the exam, to plan and act accordingly, you must have a certain discipline and make an effort of determination.

Education involves discipline. Unfortunately, the word *discipline* has acquired a negative connotation. When we talk about discipline, we automatically think of compulsory things. It is true that society imposes on us the rules by which we coexist. We understand the role of some of them, and some of them we do not. We may agree with them, or we may not. However, when we talk about our child's education, it is important that education and discipline be explained and be part of the child's motivation and his involvement.

Discipline is completed through the child's motivation and through his involvement.

Children need discipline. And they need limits established by parents. These limits provide them safety and help them to easily integrate into society. If a parent allows his child to do everything he wants, he may think that parents are indifferent to what he does. He might think, "Otherwise, why would they let me do whatever crosses my mind?!"

A total freedom does not help him at all. On the other hand, when he respects what the parent asks him and the parent shows his appreciation for this, the child feels he is valued. Even if he enjoys when you are permissive, the child senses how it discipline from you is good. Children have a peculiar sensitivity. The little children especially have very good intuition that has not yet been faded by the multitude of rules imposed by civilization.

You may say that I contradict myself. In one sentence I say that rules are necessary, and then I say that, actually, rules destroy certain qualities we are born with. Well, both statements are valid. In society we cannot have good relationships with each other if we do not have some rules that we all respect. If these rules did not exist, we would have chaos. Imagine what would happen if there were no traffic rules. An immediate traffic jam would ensue, and after that people would probably start tearing each other's hair out! How could you agree that X should pass the first if there was not a clear rule? On the other side, the numerous rules we have to respect, the sometimes overwhelming responsibilities required of us by society can fade some of the qualities we are born with. One of these qualities is intuition.

If you pay attention every time you are around a little child, you will be astonished by how many true things he says. And he will say them in a very simple way. The other day I heard a little boy aged four asking his mother, "Why is Radu so selfish?" Radu did not want in to give him a candy. He did not ask why Radu was bad—only why he was selfish. For the four-year-old child it was very clear that not sharing with others was an act of selfishness.

This concept is not very easy even for us grown-ups. I have seen so many times how grown-ups try hard to express things in a veiled way or, if possible, to avoid the truth altogether, and yet the child with his remarkable intuition goes directly to the target. In a simple and playful way you hear the naked truth from his mouth.

Returning to the child's need of discipline, the existence of some clear rules offers him safety and the feeling of being protected. Clear, firm, and constant rules, but not absurd.

The existence of some clear rules offers the child a feeling of protection and safety.

All our lives we are in a state of continuous experimentation. At the beginning of our life, when we are children, this experimentation is emphasized. Everything is new, and it has to be explored. The child does not know what may happen or what danger may come from the unknown. That is why rules offer him safety. He knows that as long as he respects what his parents tell him, nothing wrong can happen to him.

When he is little, the child tests the limits how, where, and when he can act out. It often happens that he does or says something only to carefully watch his parents' reaction. It may seem unnatural to him that his parents allow him to play on the computer at midnight, but if his parents are busy entertaining guests that night and they are more permissive, why not?

Children take advantage of the parents' weaknesses, but this does not mean that it offers them an inner comfort, too. Because within them occurs a conflict between what they know they should do and what they are doing.

Not only do little children need limitations, but the big ones do too. I met a teenager who told me that her parents trusted her very much and they had told her, "Between this limit and the other one, you can do whatever you want. It's up to you." And still she confessed to me, "But I need more guidance." And she suggested to me that these limits that were very broad were not enough as reference points in life. That she needed more direct guidance, more actual advice. And she needed help in order to handle the life situations arising from this jungle.

Her situation is very common in our present society when many parents are very busy. Sometimes we, the grown-ups, need somebody to offer us advice, to guide us, and to offer us help in order to clarify for ourselves what we have to do. Children and teenagers need this even more. How does discipline help us in life? The respect of certain rules and the existence of a certain order to our days make our lives much easier.

Rules make our life easier... provided that we accept and internalize them.

Let us observe a person who, since he was little, has been a tidy person. He will not waste time having to find his things. He will enjoy the comfort of a nice orderly environment, and he will not disturb the other members of the family with any mess left behind him. At work, he will be appreciated because he is tidy, because he always knows where a folder or a document is, and because he delivers neat work, etc. An untidy person will lose a lot of time and energy finding things he never puts in their place, and he will be a nightmare for those he lives and works with.

These examples are related to the discipline of being tidy. I do not mean to plead for perfect tidiness. On the contrary, I think that in a house where life and joy are present, things cannot always be perfectly arranged as in the army. In general, when we talk about discipline, we immediately think about a good child or a disobedient child. Discipline does not focus only on obedience to parents but also, as I said it before, the habit of doing things in a certain way: brushing teeth in the morning and in the evening, leaving things tidy before going to sleep, and not throwing things everywhere are all examples of discipline. The act of assigning a certain number of hours for studying every day, the habit of talking only after the other person finishes his or her ideas, the concept of being used to working in order to obtain something are all related to discipline.

Regarding the issue of discipline, the most important thing is that it has to be internalized by the child; otherwise, it does not have much value.

How discipline is transmitted is essential. Indeed, it is an extremely delicate aspect, because you are a human, too, and you have your own limits. And your child is an expert at testing your limits.

Discipline is carried out with love and steadiness. If you reach the phase of being angry, do your best to postpone disciplinary measures by saying something like, "We will talk later about this. Now I just want to calm down." Anger shows you are already very affected. A side of you feels hurt, and without your realizing it, your concentration has moved from the problem that needs to be solved— the disciplinary measure—to the problem of solving your affected self because your child disobeyed you. The only thing that can happen under the influence of anger is to offend and to humiliate him. Goodbye, discipline lesson!

Discipline is accomplished with love and steadiness.

In order to motivate and help your child internalize the rules you want him to learn, you must, first of all, be a role model in this respect. You cannot ask him to do something that you do completely different. You cannot ask him to eat healthy food while you eat fast food all day long.

It is good to explain to him why he must do things in one way or another, but there are also situations when the child interprets the explanations as a sign of weakness, and, then, after you have explained to him the benefits to him if he respects a rule, you must be very firm and end the discussion.

The child tends to transform your relationship with him in a relation of power. He exults when he dominates you. It is not easy, but you must reverse this relation. Not by force, but by intelligence and love.

If you succeed in staying calm in a difficult circumstance or in easily restoring your calm state, you will see that the solutions for solving the case of a conflict-ridden situation will come more easily than in a moment when you are filled with anger.

Discipline without correcting the mistake already made is not quite possible. Little children do not know when to stop—they always feel the instinctual pull of "I want"—and because of this they need discipline. The most important thing in applying a correction is that it must be equal to the child's mistake. If he made a bad grade and you forbid him to play outside for a month, his frustration will be very big. In his inner self he will know that what you do is not correct, and he will lose his trust in you and your ability to protect him.

Do not give him more punishments for the same mistake. There are parents who, for the same mistake, and not a big one, present a long list of punishments: you are not allowed anymore to play with toys for one month, to go outside, to watch TV or to play on the computer, etc. This type of excessive punishment is abnormal and upsets the child.

The correctly applied punishment has a positive value. It reduces the child's feeling of guilt because he always knows when he is wrong. But he needs to hear it from you, as the grown-up. And because, being little, he has not learned yet how to use his self-control; he needs you to do this. Punishment removes the feeling of guilt from the child's soul. But do not forget: the punishment must be proportionate to the mistake that was made.

It must not be applied when you are filled with anger, and you must continue to show him your love. Your love is for him the support that helps him overcome his punishments and other difficult moments in the educational process.

Discipline prepares the child for life, for living in society. If he did not learn to respect the laws of living in a group of people, he will quickly be taught by society to know his place or he will simply be rejected.

Punishment must be proportionate to the mistake that was made.

If you say the word "army," the first thing that comes into your mind is probably something to do with discipline—without which no battle could ever be won. This fact is valid at the individual level, too. Without strong discipline we cannot reach any goal. No matter what we want to accomplish in life, we need a plan and the power to follow it. This power results from an effort of will and action: discipline.

The peak in the positive evolution of imposed rules is represented by self-discipline. Self-discipline is an understood, internalized, and assumed discipline. Self-discipline is based on a strong wish to accomplish or to obtain something. It is based on the awareness of the fact that if you want something, you have to make a constant and planned effort to obtain it. A chaotic effort does not bring any benefit, but rather damages. It brings the inevitable disappointment that you did not get what you wanted. And, of course, it brings exhaustion without a positive result to justify it in the end.

Self-discipline is the way to accomplish your dreams, the things you want in life. Self-discipline means rigor. It means being aware of what you want, having a plan, and then acting on it. It represents the expression of a person's maturity. It is the peak of the individual development but at the same time a springboard to create more development and progress. Self-discipline is an important element of our inner life.

Discipline must have a clear purpose, a sense and logic. It must not be applied just because you are little and you do what I—the grown-up—say. It must not simply be a display of force. It must be justified by a logic the child can understand and buy into. It is the only way for him to accept and pursue it. It is the only way for the child to achieve, in time, self-discipline.

Discipline is learned. Discipline is formed. It is not something we are born with. You, as the parent, are the first to help your child travel from the externally imposed discipline to the inner discipline that will help him accomplish everything he wants in life.

Discipline is learned.
Discipline is formed.

5

Ingredients of a Happy Life

Forgiveness

The ability to forgive is the most powerful spring of our spiritual tranquility. Forgiveness brings in our soul peace and joy. When we can forgive the small or big inconveniences created by others, a lot of our struggles and worries disappear. Actually, the source of much negative energy disappears. Our feelings clear up and become calm.

The ability to forgive others is closely connected to the reconciliation with ourselves, to our self-acceptance just as we are. The inner peace and the joy come, first of all, from self-reconciliation.

**The ability to forgive
is the more powerful spring
of our spiritual tranquility.**

Self-acceptance is a point around which all our life revolves, and it is closely related to the feeling that we are accepted by our parents.

Many times parents have their own visions about the trajectory of their child's life. They dream for her to become a doctor, an economist, or a manager, to earn a lot of money, to have a family, children, and to do things in a certain way, the way they were used to. Frequently, when they ask their child to do something, they instruct her to do it in a certain way without letting the child discover her own way of doing it. And when the child is little, they impose upon her different things without even trying to obtain her involvement or to make her understand why those things are necessary. They apply a reasoning of this type: "She is little and must obey."

Mostly, all these things create in the child's soul the feeling that she is not accepted as she is, with her own wishes and personality. The child might not be aware of this feeling, but it may exist and it may give birth to different other feelings: that she is not loved, that other things are more important than she is, since her own wishes do not matter too much, that there is something wrong with her. She can experience feelings of guilt, which is why many of her actions as a child or grown-up will be directed against herself. (If we think for a moment, we will find many such behaviors that undermine our physical and psychic integrity, working to the point of exhaustion, eating unhealthy food—we know it is not good and yet we still continue eating food that adversely affects our health—insufficient rest, the skepticism that we deserve a better life, etc.)

Either ugly or beautiful, each feeling triggers another feeling of the same variety as the one that generated it, but of an even bigger size. Feelings are like a roll. They burst into our souls and trigger numerous other feelings. For example, if into the child's soul sneaks the suspicion that there is something wrong with her, then she may become more isolated, inhibited, with a very low self-confidence. This may raise her anger and fury against others. As a grown-up, she will learn how to hide these things, but they will continue existing behind the social conventions.

This is only an example. There may be any number of situations. It is important to understand that there are invisible threads that connect us to our childhood and to which we remain attached for our whole lives.

The ability to forgive springs from an attitude of openness and love for people. It intertwines with our beliefs and is hidden behind most of the feelings we experience. It comes from the depths of our being, but it is also directly related to the more or less tolerant attitude of family models. If you encourage your child to develop her own personality and you accept her just the way she is, even if she is different from you, there is a good chance that she will become a self-confident person, and from here will result many of her feelings: a general well-being, optimism, tolerance toward others, the ability to overcome small disappointments, and understanding and forgiving those who contribute to them.

Let me repeat what I mentioned at the beginning of this book: becoming a human being is a complex process. Each feature of personality is a result of the combination of many ingredients. All these ingredients go through the filter of the individual's personality. The result is a combination over which nobody can have control. All we can do, as parents, is to make sure that the ingredients we offer are good and healthy.

The forgiving attitude can become a habit. The habits of forgiving and of being tolerant are big advantages in the life for the person who displays them. Because they generate positive feelings, they are food for our soul and a balm for those who surround us. A forgiving attitude keeps you away from frustration, anger, and their consequences. The ability to forgive supposes a profound understanding of human nature.

A forgiving attitude keeps you away from frustration, anger, and their consequences.

It is possible for you to believe that if you end up forgiving everybody, then everybody will trample you. But the act of forgiving somebody who offended you does not mean having a passive attitude towards that person. You can clearly and openly communicate to him what you think, what bothered you, and what are the limits he transgressed. If the situation is serious, you can even tell him what will happen if he does it again. It is all about doing so without offending in return but, rather, with honesty and determination. Do not confuse forgiveness, however, with your efforts to clarify the situation and to keep it from happening again. Forgiveness is, first of all, a deep inner process that supposes that all the negative emotions related to the person who offended you or did something wrong to you disappears.

A gentle parent cannot raise a furious child. The child sees his parent's actions, he grows up surrounded by them, and he assimilates them. If the parent has a sympathetic attitude and shows forgiveness when somebody does something wrong to him, the child will adopt this attitude from him. The forgiving attitude does not suppose lack of steadiness—quite the contrary. The person who forgives is very clear as to why he does so, and he will show the confidence of a person who knows what he is doing.

If you love animals and you show it, then you can be sure your child will not be a person who throws stones at dogs. The child sees that you pet dogs every time you meet them. He sees that you care about them and that you feed them whenever you can, even if they are stray dogs. The child hears the warm tone of your voice when you talk to them, and he absorbs this warmth that springs from your soul. In his turn, he will do the same thing. Do not be afraid if he pulls a dog's tail from time to time when he is still little. It is a phase that will pass. He is testing the limits a little in order to see what will happen.

If you show sympathy toward people, if you do not get angry every time somebody does things differently from you, if you do not bear a grudge against somebody who tried to offend you, then your child will show the same behavior in his life, too.

Forgiveness helps us surpass the guilty feelings that sneak into our soul. Forgiveness smoothes the path we are walking on. And if our soul is peaceful, we will be able to enjoy the beautiful things in life; we will be able to be more efficient in what we do because our energy will no longer be absorbed by the negative feelings (grief, anger, etc.) and we will be able to use our energy to full capacity for beneficial purposes for our own life and for the people around us.

Forgiveness is a necessary ingredient of your child's happiness. Its permanent manifestation can transform it into a habit that will warm your child's soul. Its absence represents the presence of feelings that nobody wants but that no one knows what to do to get rid of. In the absence of a forgiving attitude, your child will be burdened with the negative emotions and suffering that spring from events that otherwise could be overcome with love and understanding. Even if your child has broken a valuable vase, if a friend has made fun of him, or if he loses a significant amount of money—all these situations lose their significance and the power to make him miserable in light of the truly important things: life itself and the joy of living it.

Forgiveness
is a necessary ingredient
of your child's happiness.

Almost all our actions become habits, and forgiveness is not an exception. It depends on us which habits we choose to grow and to transmit further to our children.

When they are little, children are like sponges. They absorb everything around them. Growing up, they try to cut a few of the invisible threads that connect them to childhood, especially when these bonds do not bring happiness to their lives. But they will never succeed in rejecting them completely. They will waste a lot of energy for rejecting something that could have been beneficial for their life.

Unconditional Love

Love is something we all aspire to experience. It is a word on everybody's lips.

Love exists, first of all, at the level of feeling, and then it acquires different manifestations in our behavior. Its existence is like a fire ball, like a huge source of heat next to which your child's heart gets warm. This source will exist for all of his life, even after you cease to exist on earth. Nothing is stronger than this feeling in our life. All of us, children and grown-ups alike, need its warm and subtle emanations. The feeling of being loved by our parents gives us emotional balance and enables our life to be balanced.

It's been said that some people are like a leaky bucket. No matter how much of the love they are looking for they receive, they are permanently frustrated because through that hole leaks everything they receive. They can never retain the love and affection they long for, even if they desperately want it. That hole in the bucket represents the absence of the feeling that you are loved. If somebody grows up as a child with the feeling that his parents do not love him, he can easily extend this to a feeling telling him that he does not deserve to be loved, that he is not worth it. And, as a grown-up, the fact that he wants to be loved will contradict the fact that he is not worth it, a well-hidden feeling in his subconscious, and in this way all he receives from an emotional point of view will leak right out of him.

The little child's ability of discernment is limited. He tends to attribute to himself the things that happen around him. If the parents argue or divorce, he may think that this happens because of him. If the parents are busy (and in our contemporary society parents are very busy) and caught in everyday chores, he may think he does not deserve their affection. The little child cannot see the world in its whole. He relates what happens to his person only. That is why, no matter how busy we are, no matter how burdened we were by our existential problems, it is necessary to always give our children the emotional support they need.

Love does not contradict discipline. In fact, if they go hand in hand, then the result will be a remarkable one. The child needs to be disciplined and, at the same time, he needs love. Discipline often involves conditioning: "After you finish your homework, you can go play." "If you are good on the visit, you will receive an ice cream." "If you are awarded at the end of the school year for grades or good behavior, we will buy you a bicycle." No matter how contingent his behaviors are on rewards or punishments, the child needs to feel your unconditional love—that you love him as he is. More or less clever, naughtier or nicer, shyer or bolder. Your love for him is not negotiable. Every moment of his life, he needs to feel that you love him. This gives him emotional safety and the power to go on, beyond the punishments and the rules he must respect.

The love for your child is not negotiable.

Love manifests itself in everything we do for our child. Both when we scold her and when we are upset. It manifests itself through our behavior, the tone of our voice, the expression on our face—especially the look in our eyes. It may also manifest itself through our simple presence. Your presence next to her when she is sad may be the support she needs to overcome the obstacle.

There are moments when the words do not help. Certain situations may be so stressful that you can do very little to help, yet your simple presence next to her, showing her that you understand his suffering and you are by her side may be enough to help her. Certainly, when the critical moment starts to fade, you can have a helpful discussion with her. The time you spend with her is proof of your love. Listening to her and giving her the opportunity to express herself is also a manifestation of your love.

Words are an important vehicle for our feelings and for the energy associated with them. This has been physically demonstrated by Masaru Emoto, who proved through repeated experiences that water changes its structure and quality after its exposure to different words. Positive words—which possess a beneficial energetic charge—such as "thank you," "love," and "gratitude" form well-shaped crystals during the freezing process, while words with a negative charge, such as "stupid" or "it's not good" form distorted and fractured crystals. Given the fact that our bodies are composed of about 70 percent water, the words we use influence us.

Words have a huge impact on us and on the people around us. Remove the words with negative charges when you speak to your child. You will notice how a warm tone in your voice and positive words can create miracles. In general, you should avoid expressions that include negative phrases, such as, "You do not want to eat?" as if you are inviting her to answer no. You can say instead: "Do you want to eat?" or "What do you want to eat?"

Out of habit, we often use such expressions as, "You don't want to go play?" "Your colleagues aren't coming?" Approaching them from a positive manner, on the other hand, is beneficial due to the positive words used and because it does not involve an answer. The choice of whether to answer or not is up to the other person.

Remove the negatively charged words when you speak with your child.

The words, along with our behavior, the tone we use, the expression we have, and, especially, along with our thoughts represent the manifestation of the feelings we have. Through all these manifestations the child feels what you transmit to him. It is in vain to say that you love him if you have just told him he is stupid, if you looked at him with hatred when you got angry, or if you did not allow him to speak when he had something to say. Beyond words, he will feel the true message.

No other thing you can offer him will ever have the value of your unconditional love. It is a precious stone he will carry in his soul forever.

The unconditional love that you offer your child will accompany him forever.

Prayer

It may seem strange, but many parents harbor feelings of anger against their children. There are even situations when parents curse their children. Their reasons may be multiple: they are not being listened to and this makes them feel they are losing control, they are afraid that their image is impaired in front of acquaintances and friends, they live with a feeling of inferiority when they do not know how to deal with their child, etc. I will not go into detail concerning these reasons—these causes that have more to do with the parents' subjective feelings than with the situation itself. It is important to point out, though, that these manifestations exist and they can harm the child very much, whether he is little or big. Between parents and children there is a strong emotional connection. There is a strong energetic connection. Words, just like parents' thoughts regarding their children, have a strong impact upon children. This impact is at a very subtle level.

A persistent annoyance of the parent with his or her own child may harm the child. All the thoughts, good or bad, that somebody has towards us affect us. When we talk about the parent-child relationship, this impact is bigger because of the strong connection between parent and child.

The other side of this coin is the good thought, the simple prayers, from the heart, of a parent for his or her child. It is the easiest way—and yet it's so important—that you can help your child. The prayer for your child should be the keystone for the beginning of every day. I'm not asking you to read prayer books. The simple, clear, and concise prayer you feel in your heart for your child may have a much bigger effect than tons of studied prayers. The prayer protects him and also helps you get rid of the fears and worries of a parent. The prayer unites your energies and may create a connection that on the level of out-loud verbal communication may have become interrupted.

I must specify a few things on prayer.

1. It is important *how* you pray.

If you have a long list with things you want in your life or in your child's life, it is necessary to choose only the most important of these. If your prayer looks like a long shopping list, there is a very small probability that all of them will be carried out. A long wish list proves, on one hand, that you are not able to establish your priorities, and, on the other, it creates within yourself a discomfort of which you may or may not be aware. For many wishes you should also consider the proverb "If you run after two rabbits, you will catch neither." Your energy is limited. If you invest it into four wishes, each will benefit from only a small fraction of your energy. But, if you choose the most important thing for you, this desire will benefit from all your energy, which will not be forced to break into pieces.

First of all, it must be very *clear* to you what you want most, for you or for your child. Then, you must put it in a manner that is very *simple*. Scratching the ear was never useful for anyone other than for buying some time. And, I do not think that you want to buy some time when you pray for your child. Rather than stringing out a long list of wishes for your child, better to say in a few simple words exactly what you want for him. Lastly, be *concise* with your prayers. If you are using prayers from a book, try a simple, clear, and concise prayer, and you will feel its strength.

2. It is important to feel the thing you are praying for.

If your prayer is only at a mental, intellectual level, it is not enough. You must vibrate at the same frequency of your desire, to *be* your desire, to feel its achievement. If you achieve this, you will feel the full blessing of God.

3. Have *faith.*

You must be convinced that God is next to you and he can hear you. And he will find a way to help you. Maybe it will not be the way you expect, but it will certainly be a helpful way. That is why, if you feel the overabundance of this faith, you may say the prayer as a gratification: "Thank you, God, for taking care of my child."

It is important how you pray for your child, what you feel when you pray, and the faith you have.

Certainly, there are countless things that we can say about prayer. That you must not pray for something that will hurt somebody else, for example. It also may happen that the thing you are praying for will not fulfilled because if it had it would do more harm to you than good.

Prayer is a good thought. It is love. It is consolation. We can use it in need, or we can integrate it into our being. We have many appropriated habits that do not honor us. Why would we refuse a habit that can make our life more beautiful? You do not need time to pray.

You only have to line up your thoughts in a certain direction. I know this is not the easiest thing with all the thoughts that swarm in our heads and deplete our energy. With the help of prayer you can capture all thoughts into one and enjoy the provided peace. You can create a circle of beneficial energy in the middle of which you and your child live.

You must vibrate at the same frequency of your desire, to *be* your desire, to feel its achievement.

Values

People need values. Without them they would operate at the level of animals. What generates this need is our conscience, without which man would not differentiate between good and bad deeds. Values make our life beautiful; they help us define our personality and obtain our self-esteem.

When we are little, we take over our parents' values. Because they are the closest to us, their world is our universe from where we absorb everything, trying to define our personality in relation to them. When you are little, your parents' universe is the moral and the aesthetic reference point to which you relate. Many of the values that surrounded you in your childhood are deeply infiltrated in your personality and they push you, all your life, to act in one direction.

The values we carry within us and upon which we rely for our existence are not indifferent to us. They are not neutral in relation to us. They influence everything we do, the way we think, and our feelings. We can say that the path to happiness is paved with our values. Values are transmitted from generation to generation, and they illuminate our life regardless of our age. The absence of values means the lack of equilibrium and support in search of our identity;

it means a life full of anxieties and failures. Without them, the human being would not be able to blossom or reach his or her potential. The values I want to talk about are approached from the perspective of the individual benefit and not the collective. The collective good comes naturally if every individual is happy.

1. Simplicity. Simplicity is a value that I, personally, appreciate and love very much. If people would discard the burden of unnecessary things, starting with useless material goods accumulated only as a result of a psychological dependence and not of their utility and including worrying about unessential things in their existence, life would show itself to be brighter and fuller.

Many things, generated by the engine of a consumerist society, overwhelm us vainly. Because of too many false appearances we are not able to see the essential things. Our life becomes more difficult every day as new products enter the market, increasingly modern products, that make us want them and that we do not always need but for which we are ready to sacrifice the most important thing we have: our time, in essence, our life. We live our life in a rush, and we forget to enjoy the little simple things that actually constitute the essence of a fully lived life.

Enjoy a walk in the open air with your child, breathe together the strong air of spring, admire with him the stars in the sky, live the joy of being with him; these will be the warm moments that will enrich his soul, that he will remember later and that he will relive many times. You can do many things in support of simple joys. You can give up the second TV set from your house for a trip to the mountains; you can give up a fabulous dinner for a dinner that's simple but full of joy. If at a dinner where you have different sorts of food, your attention will be focused on the food; at a simple dinner you can focus on your child, on being together and enjoying your dinner. When I speak about simplicity, I speak about a moderate life in the context of a society predisposed to consumption much bigger than its needs. I do not mean poverty. It is difficult to taste a simple dinner when you live in a stricken poverty. I speak about simplicity as a state of equilibrium, as a balance between abundance for the sake of abundance and moderation for the sake of a healthy and fulfilled life.

Simplicity takes us to the essence of life and to its joy. A simple and to-the-point communication reaches its purpose much quickly than any complicated expression. Real communication means that your message must reach and be understood by the person you send it to.

There are many children for whom, nowadays, Christmas means treats. Actually, not only for the children, but for the grown-ups, too, Christmas has come to be a big party and an opportunity to over-stuff ourselves. The essential spiritual aspects of this holiday become lost: communion with others, the forgiveness of sins over the year, and the sharing of the joy of being and of making things together. The greatest joy comes from the involvement and the participation of everybody, old and young, in the preparation of this holiday. In many houses, this holiday can be a tedious task for the housekeepers, and especially because we feel if we lay on the table only two or three dishes, we are not doing as much as other people or as much as people expect from us so we make more and more. The tendency is to fill the table with all sorts of food, an opportunity of pride that we have all the things that lie on the table and that we are missing nothing. Little by little, the spiritual feelings disappear, and the culinary excesses are paid in extra pounds, in discomfort, and even in a damaged health.

Enjoying the simple joys next to your child means he will never experience them without feeling their thrill. He will not be able to ignore them. From these experiences he will acquire the power to go on.

2. Honesty. Honesty begins with you. Nobody can be honest with others if, first of all, they are not honest with themselves. To be honest means using the same measure for your judgment of yourself as for others. It means to detach yourself from your own interest and put yourself above it. First of all, honesty brings inner comfort, equilibrium, and peace of mind. Secondly, all people want others to be fair to them. They want fair relationships, especially an honest couple relationship and a child who tells the truth. The question is, can you be fairly treated if you are not fair yourself?

Many years ago I took part in an episode where a mother encouraged her daughter, a teenager, to take advantage financially of her relationship with boys, meaning go out and have fun with them at their expense and then abandon them. I wondered, then, what would that girl's expectations be for her life partner? She will probably want to be treated fairly while the list of her own bad-faith actions will be erased from her mind by the justifications we all find when it comes to our own behavior.

When you expect honesty from others, look deeply in your soul and see if you offer what you expect from them. You cannot want a beautiful life and at the same time put at its foundation lies and deceptions because life does not work like this. Life has its own unalterable laws, and no matter how much you want it to be otherwise it is not you who makes those laws.

Parents tend to put their child's best interests above the well being of others. But your child's best cannot be separated from other people's best. If you, as parent, direct your child, willingly or unwillingly, toward a personal gain at the expense of others, you place him on a path where he will never be really happy. Because the relationship where I win and you lose represents a false gain. If we make it specific and we refer to the couple relationship, because most people look for their happiness in this arena, think whether you have ever seen a happy person next to an unhappy one.

Honesty is the foundation of the values pyramid. You can hold many other values, but if the base has cracks everything will quake from time to time and it will reorganize the structure until you are ready to admit the truth to yourself.

The child learns from his parent to be fair and have goodwill toward other people. The parent is his first model. Certainly the models from school will come later, from life, from his group of friends. But there is a strong foundation upon which all these things settle, and this is the foundation that you provide him.

3. Compassion. Compassion is the most beautiful and the most complex feeling that can warm people's souls. Complexity results from the understanding of other people, of the situation where another person is and of his feelings; from the honesty without which you cannot experience this feeling; from love; but also from the gesture of affection itself. This gesture may be a consolation, a charity, or even a good word. Anything that shows the one suffering that he is not alone.

Compassion lived and shown with honesty is like a flame warming your soul; it is a flame that does not burn you but protects you from the negative things in your life. No matter how upset you may be, an act of compassion toward you balances your feelings. When you give something from all your heart, the boundary between you and the person you offer compassion to disappears. You feel the other person's suffering, and at the same time you feel the effect of your love toward the person close to you in the form of a good feeling that warms your heart. There are people around whom you feel fantastic just because you see in their eyes that they understand you and they understand your suffering. And this is enough for you.

Compassion is a feeling but also a value that comes from inside us, but it also needs to be sown and taken care of. The education received from parents and school is very important for the implantation of this value.

When I was attending primary school, the teacher started a service project for an old woman who lived near the school. She was all alone and had very little money. Each student brought from home what he could afford: sugar, oil, flour, anything was welcomed. We did these collections a few times. Being a child, I did not realize how much that support mattered to that old woman, and I even felt a slight discomfort when interacting with the strong smell of the old things in that house. And still, that action had such a strong echo over the years that I tend to believe it was one of the seeds from which germinated the feeling of compassion within me.

Many things from childhood had this effect upon me. If I think about my passion for gardening and everything nature means, and I look back over the years, I replay all the actions that inspired me: my old aunt who lived around the same courtyard as I and who took care of her garden from morning till night and whose flowers and smells were a delight for my senses every day; the tree we planted in the schoolyard during an activity teaching us about nature; my father's joy when we used to arrive at our garden, a place on the edge of the lake where I felt like in heaven. At that time I had no idea that my aunt, hunchbacked by work, and her garden would have such an influence on me. It is only now that, if I close my eyes, I know the place of every flower from her garden, and this makes me realize how much that meant to me.

Childhood is like the field in spring. You sow, you sow, but only after you harvest the crop will you know if the seeds were good, if they matched with the soil, if they had enough sunlight and water.

The feeling of compassion is cultivated. The child sees his parents and how they take care of the old and ill grandfather, how they caress a dog on the street and take him to the shelter, how they jump to help a neighbor in need, or how they say a good word to their workmate. The child internalizes all these behaviors, these feelings, and when the right time comes, he will manifest them. Of course, it is important that parents act like this permanently and not only from time to time so that this feeling germinates in the child's soul.

Compassion is also a beneficial value for society, through its effects, but at the individual level, the benefits are even greater because the individual is the one who enjoys this feeling. I have noticed, over time, however, a reaction of rejection of this feeling at times from people in suffering: "Do not pity me, please!" they may say. And there are a few things to be said on this issue.

If you help somebody with a sense of arrogance and from the height of your position you condescend to look down at the one in need, this is not compassion at all. Besides, many people reject help out of pride, which is more than silly. You need help, you need to be helped out, and yet you still reject that help because your self does not allow you to because in your mind you think that, if you are helped, this means you are inferior to the other person. Mutual help is natural both when you offer it and when you receive it. Pride has no place in this situation. When you are in trouble or you have a need you cannot handle alone, it is fantastic to see that somebody helps you without any interest but only because he understands your need.

4. Self-esteem. With every point you impose on your child, just because he is little or just because at this moment you are more powerful, you take a little from his self-esteem. You show lack of respect for his being and for his ability to understand things if you educate him by force and obtrusion. In our society too many parents use this type of educational perspective. The child learns self-respect from his parents' attitude toward him. They are his initial reference points.

Self-esteem is an important pawn in the evolution of the child's personality. According to the dose of this esteem, other features of personality will be outlined, and the child, a future grown-up, will be pushed to act in one direction or another. The trust in his ability to accomplish the things he wants depends on his self-esteem; having a job that will make him happy or a beautiful and lasting relationship will also depend on his self-esteem.

All our life revolves around our self-esteem: our inner tranquility, the confidence that we can do certain things, the more optimistic or more pessimistic vision we have of life.

Self-esteem is a guide on our spiritual and material way. It is the main point around which all our life is spinning. In it lies our faith that we deserve or not to be happy. It evolves during our life depending on our actions and on their results. Its starting point is in our parents' attitude toward us at the beginning of our life. The confidence the parents show in our ability to understand and do things, the way they correct our mistakes or they convince us to do the things that they consider good represents the starting point of our self-esteem.

A lack of self-esteem may lead to self-destructive actions, to inferiority complexes, to distrust our own selves, to a way of thinking anchored from the beginning in a negative point of view.

It is difficult to believe that somebody who does not respect himself could respect others. The respect for others, as the love for them, is a mirror of self-esteem. The stronger the self-esteem, the bigger the ability to respect others.

You are certainly tempted to think of the situations when you cannot relate to your little child, and, more or less, you must impose upon him certain things, bedtime, for example. I go back now to what I have said in the chapter about discipline. You can force a child to do something that you want in many ways. After you extend his playtime by one hour because he does not want to go to bed, you can take him by the arm and throw him on the bed, shouting, "That is it! I cannot do it anymore. It is enough. Now go to bed." All this action becomes traumatic for both of you. Or you can say to him in a firm way, from the moment you decided to let him play one more hour, "I will let you play for one more hour. Then you will go to bed." The act of showing him understanding means a lot to the child. Even five more minutes to play can make him happy. If we do it without pity, without taking into account his wishes, if we impose ourselves just because we are the grown-ups and he is only a child whose duty is only to listen, then he is traumatized, and his self-esteem lowers dramatically.

This is only an example. The situations where parents impose their points of view are plentiful. We tend to decide what is good for them and how to impose our point of view. Sometimes, some parents do this even when the child is already an adult. They resort to a psychological and moral blackmail that they have invoked all their life: "If you marry X, I will never talk to you again!" There is nothing worse than forcing your child to make such a choice: the choice between you, the one who raised him, and his happiness, as he sees it at that moment.

5. Tolerance. I have talked about tolerance in detail in the chapter on forgiveness. I will not repeat what I have said there, but I do not want to neglect this big human value from the collection of values that need to be cultivated first of all for the individual advantage and then for the social one.

Tolerance is a measure of love, a measure of dedication, of understanding the humanity within us. Tolerance shows our understanding toward the fact that people are different; they think, they observe, and they act differently from one another without meaning that what each other thinks is wrong. Tolerance is a big inner smile through which you enjoy people as they are, with those qualities that are good and maybe less good.

By cultivating this value in your child, you offer him the joy of life, the joy of tasting everything beautiful life can offer him.

Tolerance is a big inner smile through which you enjoy people as they are.

6. Love. Love does not only mean affection for parents, for children, for life partners, or for everything that has a direct connection to us. Love is a state of mind. It is the state when we feel pure, untouchable, and illuminated by divine grace. It is the state when we do not need anything from the outside but only to keep the light that floods our soul. In this state of grace we feel emotionally balanced, powerful through the inner force of good, and capable of offering others around us a piece from our wealth.

Raising your child in the spirit of love means lighting the fire that will glow his entire life. Any gesture of love and dedication he does for somebody else will have a tenfold effect upon him, spreading in his soul the harmony and joy of life.

If you have doubts regarding this aspect, look carefully at the faces of people who offer you, no matter what, a smile, a gesture, a material thing, without having a personal interest in it. Watch them carefully and you will see their face shining from a special light; their entire being is a spring of joy and fulfillment. No matter how tired and upset we may be, we always find our balance in a gesture of love. Because this is a natural state of our soul toward which we tend with or without realizing it. Love is the greatest healer of our soul. Any spiritual problem you may have, love is the full remedy. And any physical ailment can be overcome more easily when you are surrounded by love. Love exists within us as a condition of our existence. Experiences may overcome us, and social conventions may cover it. Your duty as parent is to protect the core of love in your child's soul and to nurture it with all those things that help it grow and blossom. Because nobody, no human being, will ever feel accomplished without this core to bear fruit inside him.

Love is the greatest healer of our soul.

Do not mistake someone's success with the feeling of accomplishment. Yes, you may feel accomplished when you are successful, but then you need another success and then another one. Love is about the accomplishment of the soul not of the intellectual or the self. Love manifests through every gesture you make. Both when you plant a flower and when you patiently wait for an old man to cross the street without shouting at him to get out of the way or pushing past him. Love is also when you do not jump to criticize your workmate when he does things differently from everyone else and when you contemplate a landscape that your heart enjoys.

There may be people who do not understand this feeling simply because they have never experienced it, because they have not seen it around them. There is no fault in this. The experience of love may start with a simple gesture: offer something to a person who needs that particular thing without you gaining something from it, for example. You will see how the other person's joy will flood your soul, too. Try to be kinder with the people around you without exaggerating, and you will see that, first of all, you will feel better.

If you educate your child in the school of love, you free him from many bad things.

He will be less tempted to judge others and strain his mind and soul, and he will have more energy to invest in really creative things. As I have said before, our energy is limited. We may occupy it with thoughts and actions that destroy our soul and body or we may invest it in positive things that are beneficial for our life and for others.

He will experience a much greater inner freedom because many times this freedom is restricted by our own thoughts, by judgments of value and beliefs. Eleanor Roosevelt said, "No one can make you feel inferior without your consent." When a person learns the lesson of love, he or she is above all things, and nothing can touch him or her. The bigger your love, the smaller and forceless the beliefs and the judgments that restrict your freedom. Imagine two fighters in a field. That field is you, your mind and soul. When love takes one step ahead, all bad things draw back and shrink from the field. If you let the fire of love die, all the fears and the bad thoughts will invade and will destroy your soul. The true freedom is the inner one, and it is rendered, at the end, by a state of wellness, of quietness and of love.

A child will live by tasting all the wonderful things that can be experienced in this life.
He will know how to enjoy his own creations, but also those of the universe. The world and the life will appear to him in all their beauty.

6

Moral laws
we cannot transgress

Fear

> *The fated will happen.*
> *Gaelic Proverb*

Fear is one of man's greatest enemies. Fear, in all its shapes, old, general, regarding the future, regarding what has happened to other people, regarding poverty, death, and even life. Some political leaders and extremists have always ruled through fear, and they deeply implant in our being the fear of doing something that could be punished by the system; some religious leaders, as well, operate the same way, making us fear God and thereby controlling our behavior.

Life lived under the empire of fear estranges us from ourselves and from the possibility to joyfully live our life. Fear makes us behave differently from how we feel, and it does not allow us to show our real being. For fear that they will be misunderstood, people act, many times, the opposite from how they want to. For example, a person may choose not to help an old man who can barely cross the street for fear this will appear as a sign of weakness or as a childish and laughable thing because nobody does such a gesture anymore, and, in this context, the gesture may seem almost silly. Fear forces us to make wrong decisions, such as marrying someone just from the desire to eliminate the feeling of insecurity in future, and, in this way, those who make this step condemn themselves to an unhappy life.

Fear, no matter the shape it takes, makes us incapable of enjoying life, even if there are no imminent dangers; rather, it brings us close to the things that scare us because the more we run away from them, the faster they catch up to us. An old saying refers to the fact that the fated will happen, and, if we pay attention, we will realize we have heard it many times before. Actually, it is something we all have experienced in certain circumstances: the more afraid we are of something, the bigger the probability that thing will manifest itself in our life. And here we come back to the thoughts that create our life.

If you fear illness very much, the probability that you will attract it in your life is great. If you are afraid that your life partner will betray you, sooner or later this will happen. If you think about skipping an hour from work in order to take care of some personal problems, and you fear that your boss will see you, at that very moment, even if many days had passed without you two seeing each other, at that moment it is very probable that you will meet him. A life lived under the empire of fear is actually the life living us. We are not managing our own life, but rather the fear is managing our life. In its name most decisions are made to the detriment of the uniqueness within us. You can no longer be spontaneous because fear paralyzes you. The fear domination has repercussions throughout the deepest aspects of your life.

A life lived under the empire of fear is actually the life living us.

Fear can be of different types. It is okay to be afraid in a situation when you really are in danger. If one evening, when you come home from work, you are attacked by a band of punks in the street the fear helps you summon your resources and do something for yourself: to call for help, to run, to fight, etc. If it is manifested into normal limits it has benefits: to put you on guard for potentially dangerous situations and to summon your resources to save yourself, for example. But this is not the fear that destroys our lives. Most of the time, it is a fear without an object, what we call anxiety, or a fear disproportionate to the object that generated it.

We perceive the surrounding reality through the emotions we live. If we permanently live in a general state of fear—or if we have an optimistic nature—then we will change the reality according to our feelings. If, for example, you go to an exam and you think that if you do not pass it you will embarrass yourself in front of your colleagues or you do not believe in yourself that you will pass it, then it is slightly probable that you do not pass it. Either your memory will play tricks on you or you will not remember the information although you learned it or you will be so distracted by all these preoccupations you will not be able to focus on the exam itself. You have probably met, too, the type of people who do not study very much but go to the exam "at random," thinking what could happen more than failing it—and, guess what, they pass it. And you have studied to death and you failed it while your colleague with that nonchalance that you will never be able to prove passed the exam.

Anxiety is the most common shape of fear that we see in society, as it can be lived at different intensities and it can do real damage to a person's inner life. Most conspicuously, it is related to the social area with social relationships, with self-image and the way we are seen by the others. Beyond biological factors, the environment where the child is growing and also her parents' attitude and behaviors may create a foundation for the manifestation of the anxiety in a person's life. A secure environment, where love and protection are offered to the child, keeps her away from fears without an object. The child's safety, both emotional and physical, helps her watch life with confidence and optimism. And when you regard life with confidence, it answers you back accordingly with more confidence.

When you regard life with confidence, it answers you back accordingly with more confidence.

On the other hand, too much protection is not good either. A hyper-protective environment creates a lack of confidence for the child and for her abilities to solve problems. If, for example, a fearful parent accompanies his or her child to school until the age of adolescence, fearing that she could get hurt by something, then the child will develop distrust in herself and in her ability to manage different situations. She may also have a strong addiction to the parent, which later may turn into an addiction to someone else. Do not protect your child more than she needs. She must feel she is loved, but she must also feel she can manage different challenges of life, in accordance to her age.

For example, it is difficult to say what age the child should be to go to school alone. It depends on the child's personality, on how far away the school is, on how many means of transportation she must change to get there, on how safe the neighborhoods are, etc. That is why the decisions must be made depending on the context. If you send the child to school to early, for example, if she is in kindergarten and must walk a long way, you can traumatize her. If you accompany her to school until she is fifteen years old, you can certainly inhibit her and make her addicted to you.

These things are very delicate, and if you feel overwhelmed, you may ask some advice from a professional. A psychologist can help you make a decision. But you can also solve the situation by exploring experimenting. First, you can explain the idea to your child and see how she reacts. You may be surprised, and she may be thrilled to go alone or with a classmate to school. Or you may, at first, at the end of the school day not wait for her in front of the school, but just go toward her. In this way, she will take the first step by herself, feeling safe that you are close. It will be a real adventure for her.

Many parents threaten their child, even nowadays, with warnings such as, "the boogeyman will get you if you are not good," or with other characters that scare the child. And all these are in order to force her to do something she does not want to do willingly. Many times the tired and tedious parents turn to a threat of punishment in order to get the child's obedience. But the effects of the threat are devastating on a psychological level. To obtain something by force or by fear from your child means opening the door for her future anxieties. Truly, it is not easy to obtain from her what you want, especially when you consider you are only doing it for her own good and she becomes more stubborn than a donkey. You need to correctly evaluate the situation before finding a solution. You may eliminate a wish from the list—you will certainly find something.

It is said that fear gives birth to monsters. These monsters find shelter within us, eating our inner tranquility and limiting the expression of ourselves. Do not plant the fear in your child's soul just because you wish to secure her entire life (or to control her life). Teach her how to protect herself from possible dangers. It is safer to teach her this thing than to scare her. The most efficient way to fight against her fears and anxieties is to enjoy life along with her. Joy and gladness fight against the fears that tend to nest in the child's soul. Be careful with the things you say around her, with the stories that spin around her and whose dramatic endings may ignite both her imagination and fear.

Do not make use of your child's fears in order to control her or to manipulate her emotions. Statements like, "If I die, the dogs will eat you!" said only from the parents' desire to obtain more appreciation are of no use for anyone, including the person who says such lines. The child has a stronger ability to visualize and imagine than the grown-up. For her the word translates quicker in an image and imagination can work without limits.

If you are not convinced of all these things, make an inventory of all your fears and worries. Try to write them on a piece of paper and then imagine how life could look without them. Do you feel how you could clear your life of them? Do you feel how beautiful your life is and all the things you see, you feel, you hear, and you taste from it?

Most fears relate to potential events, things we are afraid could happen in a future more or less distant. The things we are afraid of are in the future, and we cannot know for sure that they will happen, but the *fear* we feel is in the present. And, actually, we live in the present through fear of all those things that have not happened yet. And, one way or another, by thinking or doing them, we attract them in our life. That is why we say, "The fated will happen."

Do not scare the child in order to control her or to manipulate her emotion.

If there are concrete events where you must protect your child from something, like an earthquake, thieves, aggressors, illness, the danger of hurting herself falling from a height, etc., then teach her the ways to protect herself from these events. Certainly, you will not be able to control the events. And you should do this in a way that will make her feel safe because she knows all these things, not in a way that will make her scared of what may happen to her.

Anger

We meet furious people all the time. In the street, at work, in our group of friends, in the family and—why not admit it—each of us had had this feeling at one time or another. Anger comes with an emotional charge that burns you inside; it is like a volcano that, once it starts to erupt, cannot be stopped and nobody knows when it is going to end. Anger clouds your mind; it destroys any trace of reason and tolerance, forcing you to make wrong decisions and hurt others unwillingly. Anger is one of the most destructive emotions and among the most harmful to out health. The habit of living within this state can even contribute to certain diseases, especially heart diseases. The main pillars that support anger are a person's ego and his or her desire to keep a certain image. And sometimes things happen through no fault of our own and we may feel ourselves growing angry without meaning or wanting to. No matter the causes that generates the anger, anger has physical consequences. Anger takes energy from us and causes a strong inner discomfort, and it almost always brings an imbalance to our relationship with others.

Many times how anger affects you is related to what you learn from your family and the way anger manifests itself in those who surround you. It is highly unlikely to see a person who is often furious person or who never shows understanding toward others come from a calm family. On one hand, it is about the lessons a person receives, and on the other it is about the types of behavior a person sees and appropriates for him or herself. At this moment, we are not talking about the anger or frustration of small children who just want to test their parents' limits. I refer here to the parents' behavior and educational principles that set the foundation for the presence or absence of anger in the life of the future grown-up.

A child's anger is temporary, and although children must be treated with understanding, parents do not have to give the child what he wants during a tantrum because this will do nothing but confirm to him that through this manifestation he can get whatever he wants from the people around him. When a child shouts, cries, and does everything to obtain what he really wants, the best method is to look at him with understanding and calmly tell him that you will talk to him and try to help him only after he calms down. It must be very clear to him that he will not get anything from you from a tantrum or any other outburst of anger or frustration.

But, as I mentioned, the child's anger is not the main subject here, rather the parents' education that feeds or, on the contrary, cuts the roots of the anger's manifestation in the later life of the grown-up.

Yes, being a parent it is not the easiest job on earth. I do not think there is anything in this world that could keep us from never being angry or showing anger. But if the furious manifestations are frequent in the parents' behaviors, then the probability for those to appear at some point in the life of the child who becomes a grown-up are very high. It goes without saying that you cannot counteract such manifestations in your child's life if you yourself are demonstrating them on a regular basis.

What are the principles of action to counteract the manifestations of the anger in your child's life? Your **behavior** is the first thing you must take care of. Your model of behavior is an essential reference point in the child's life.

Your attitude toward other people. Teach your child to look at people with softness, to understand that people are different and that is why their actions and reactions will be different. This does not mean that one acts well and another bad but only that their actions are different, and as long as they do not hurt anybody, people are free to behave as they want.

Self-image. Help your child have a good self-image and not depend on others. Help him be aware of himself and of his value.

Many times, the education given by parents and the education offered by the child's school and by society create within the child an addiction to the approval and praise of others. And then the child will run after the recognition of others, allowing himself to be influenced by others and their opinion of him. People will have their own opinion about things. That is their problem. If you know who you are and are comfortable in your own skin, this is the most important thing.

Self-image is one of the pillars that can support anger. If a person's self-image is not strong, is apt to waver, and changes depending on what someone else says, it can become fuel for the manifestation of the anger in your life. If the self-image is strong and healthy—and it is real, authentic, and not fake in any way—then the anger will pack up and go away, leaving space in your child's psyche for other feelings that will lighten his load in life.

Many times the education offered by parents, school, and society create within a child an addiction to the approval and praise of others.

Certainly, beyond the family perimeter, the child can see the anger manifestations around him. Indeed, there is the danger that he perceives this as a proof of power, and he may want to manifest them, too. You will be able to counteract this effect through your educating him, observing him, and explaining to him every time you have the chance the manifestations around him. From the day your child is born, you have eighteen years at your disposal to set the foundation for a beautiful and accomplished life.

Guilt

To err is human.

There is a custom, quite widespread among parents, to make their children feel guilty. There is not from a sadistic pleasure within the parent but rather a way through which the parent tries to influence his or her child to learn the difference between right and wrong and offer her a moral education. Sometimes it may also be an attempt to manipulate the child's feelings in order to secure her love and respect. But guilt is not the best way to impart a moral education or to win the child's respect.

If you want to offer your child a moral education, show her the consequences of good and bad deeds. Help her understand them. Be a model of humanity for her. If she makes a mistake, which is normal for a child, explain to her why she was wrong and the consequences of her deeds. Show her understanding because any of us can make a mistake and explain to her that the most important thing is that she learns from it and not make the same mistake the second time. If the mistake is repeated or is very serious, you may find a punishment according to the mistake, but be aware of the fact that the punishment's role is double: to make the child become aware that there are consequences for everything she does and to remove, psychologically speaking, therapeutically, the feeling of guilt.

Guilt does not help you, it does not stimulate you to go forward, to do things better, to try to solve anything. On the contrary, it throws obstacles in your way and creates obstructions at the mental level. It is like a label you carry that tells yourself and others that you are helpless. Maybe the event happened a long time ago, but you keep wearing the guilt for the rest of your life—and sometimes all of this for something that is of minor significance in the grand scheme of things.

Guilt can limit
your child's evolution.

Guilt is a worm that gnaws the soul without helping it in any way. It brings with it worries, fears, and frustrations for things that can no longer be changed. It is not constructive for us to feel guilty— what does move us forward, however, is to realize we were wrong, see if there is anyway to repair the mistake, and/or determine that we will not repeat it again. It is important to go on, to continue the way for our progress and not go backward. Guilt may arrest a person's evolution because it can keep him blocked in the trap of useless feelings.

The feeling of guilt goes hand in hand with a negative self-image, which further brings additional damages to that person.

As I have said in the chapter about forgiveness, the child may also feel guilty for things that have nothing to do with him. If his mother and father argue with each other, he may think they do it because of him. Many children feel guilty when their parents divorce. Many parents may, in fact, fight because of the children, but this happens because he is important to them and because they may have different points of view concerning his education. Guilt is cultivated unconsciously by his parents, from their desire to offer a code of moral behavior to the child. Torn by frustrations, a person cannot offer to himself or to others around him the best of what he has to offer.

Show your child that you make mistakes, too. Admit when you are wrong and show him with determination what you are going to do so that it does not happen again. When you admit your mistake and you accept it, you can also get beyond it, and, thereby, your life may go on without remaining blocked between feelings of guilt. Do not overwhelm your child with guilty feelings—at the same time be careful that you do not allow your child to get away with bad behavior as if nothing happened. This is another unhealthy extreme.

Envy and Hatred

Set aside what is yours.

People do not realize how much they harm they do, first of all themselves, through the feelings of envy and hatred. Envy and hatred are destructive to others, but they do even more harm to the person concerned. They create anxiety and send you away from what is good in you. Instead of sleeping contented in your bed at night, you toss and turn, tormented by thoughts and feelings that do not bring you any advantage.

The envious person focuses on what the other has instead of focusing on his own person and seeing what he can do with the gifts he has. A person animated by hatred will chase only destructive actions and may end up destroying even the good things that he's done and has.

It is important to inspire your child with self-confidence and with confidence in his abilities. But this confidence does not have to come from comparison to somebody else but only from the sincere appreciation for the qualities he has. Comparing your child to another child will make him permanently look at another person's yard and feel good and appreciated only if he has better a better one. He must be aware of the fact that "we set aside what is ours." There is a lot of wisdom in this proverb that tells us that every being is unique, that every man and woman has his or her own way to follow, and that you do not have to take from someone else in order to have something. Our true richness is our inner treasure, and nobody can take that away. This is the spirit of an education: concerning ones relationship with others in society on one side and on the other side a personal education without which your child cannot be happy.

Pride

Pride is a "sin" that sends you away from the essence of your being and that ruins a lot of relationships between people. It is a feeling that places yourself above the others. It makes you feel superior to the person you are having a conflict with or feel you are wronged, and instead of trying to solve the situation, you end a relationship or an experience that could actually bring you benefits.

Pride supposes inflexibility, false superiority, and self-sufficiency, and it may lead you to waste unsuspected opportunities. Out of pride you may refuse a sincere helping hand, and you may plunge deeper into a problematic situation. Out of pride you may refuse to cooperate with a colleague or life partner, and in this way the problem may deepen, leading to a permanent break. Out of pride you cannot admit you were wrong; out of pride you may refuse to make a humanitarian gesture.

Pride can make you lose a lot not only in your social and work life but also opportunities. And in this case, as in others, your behavior model as a parent is essential. The way you act will be a source of inspiration for your child.

Critical Judgment

For many people, criticizing others has become a habit. Even if it does not affect them personally, even if it has nothing to do with them, people still feel a need to expose their opinion about other people's behavior and choices. Unfortunately, the criticism is not fair most of the time and is subjective and shallow.

People judge others for their actions without knowing the situation or context that led to those actions. When we act, people do not know our inner motivations. They hasten to judge without even trying to understand the whole picture. Every action has a context, and the two cannot be separated. For example, X may speak very loudly because she has a grandmother who cannot hear very well and living next to her, she is used to speaking like that. When she is not close to her grandmother, she may continue to speak loudly without realizing it, and, doing so, she may be disturbing to others and be considered rude.

Or, as another example, expressing your point of view is welcomed, but if you do it by violating someone else's right to reply or by interrupting the person and not allowing him or her to expound on their ideas, then it is not a positive thing anymore.

Psychologically, by criticizing others, a person tries to put herself on a superior rung to others. But such superiority is false and rings true only in the mind of the person who does the criticizing. Sometimes, however, the person has a sense telling her what she is doing or saying is not quite right, but she ignores it; the desire to dominate through superiority is stronger than the desire to understand the other person. The biggest problem of judging others is that it affects interpersonal relationships and affects the person who judges.

Reckless judgment darkens the human being and opens the door for negative feelings. A shallow and reckless judgment may be the spark for lighting anger within a person. Excessive and subjective criticism only destroys and is in direct opposition to finding solutions. When we realize someone's flaws, it is good not to tell them just to show how smart we are. If it is necessary at all—and usually it is not— offer constructive criticism in a way as detached and objective as possible, underlining first of all the person's positive aspects. Most of the time it's best only to notice in silence because many times a person is not ready for a change; our criticism will not bring that person any benefit and in fact may very likely hurt his or her feelings.

You may ask yourself what this has to do with your child. Well, his happiness, his inner balance and harmony depend on the judge inside him and his ability to understand others. The more he respects other people's way of feeling, thinking, and acting, the more complete his state of well being will be.

The person who severely judges the people around him will never be satisfied with himself because that inner judge will be merciless not only with others, but with himself as well.

Man is a unique being. We are so alike so different from one another all at the same time. On the inside we experience similar thoughts, but the way they flow and the connection between them, their intensity, and their manifestation in concrete actions are so different! Doing things differently does not mean a person is bad or wrong. It relates, rather, to the person's ability to express himself. Society tends to encourage uniformity among us at the expense of our self-expression.

As the parent, your duty is to help your child respect the rules of society by understanding the meaning and purpose of these rules, on one side, and to help him find out ways of expressing the unique being within him in light of these rules.

Your duty is to help him understand that people are unique beings and not to judge others through the lens of his own beliefs or experiences.

Otherwise, his happiness will be prejudiced, and his expectations that people behave and think similarly to the way he thinks will be met by disappointments.

About "Sins" and Their Consequences

All these feelings—fear, guilt, envy, etc.—represent "sins" because they stop human beings from having harmonious and loving lives. Men and women cannot fully enjoy their lives or the people around them if they are too busy criticizing or being displeased with something.

Each of these feelings represents a barrier to your child's happiness and suffering for those around him. None of them is helpful for his spiritual evolution. Through education, especially the education he receives at home, these feelings may be polished, adjusted, and even defeated. They are a part of human nature because we let them be, for different reasons. That is why your role as parent is to fight against these potential "sins" and to make room in your child's life for the ingredients that can lead him to a happy and bright existence.

7

Parenting

Follow Your Intuition

No matter how much information you may have on what is good for your child, no matter how much you read about the topic, the best way for her is what passes through your soul. No statistics and no book, however complex, can tell you who your child is. Only you, with the heart of a parent, know that. Lend your ear to what parent's intuition tells you and do not allow supposed rules, dogmas, and principles to obscure it.

The connection between you and your child is strong and built for a lifetime, indestructible.

It started with your desire to have a child and is endless.

Listen to your intuition!

Throughout your evolution as parent you will encounter many popular opinions and trends on the best way to raise a child. You will encounter many techniques on how to obtain what you want from her. Do not forget that no method, however good it may be and no matter how many results it could have offered in time, can be applied just like that and guarantee results; it has to be adjusted both according to the child's personality and to the context of the situation. Judge each instance according to your heart.

A Lifetime Experience

Being a parent is a unique experience. It is an experience that exceeds the strict boundaries of raising and educating a child. It is an act of creation, an act of intense living, a process of becoming in which you evolve together with your child.

What you are will reflect upon him and what he is will reflect upon you. Your personality and your behavior will influence him in one direction or another. His actions will echo in your soul. Everything that he does will have consequences for you. And, still, do not forget you are two distinct lives. Do not focus on your child in a way that obstructs the evolution of your own life. Grow together with him as the branches of a tree do. This growth refers to everything you want to do in your life, to your aspirations but, especially, to your inner road because from here everything begins: from the inside to the outside. Your evolution is, first of all, an act of inner experience, a war with yourself that you have won.

Human evolution, above all, is an act of inner experience.

Let me add one more thing. Do not assume a position of superiority to your child because you have many things to learn from him. A child is without preconceptions and is more open to see things as they are than a grown-up. Many times his perception can be clearer than yours, so do not ignore it.

Being a parent involves the greatest miracle of life: giving birth to another being! What can be more wonderful? If we look at the animal world, nothing moves us more than a pair of mates and its babies. I have seen in amazement how sparrow parents stirred above the bush where their baby fell while it was trying to fly. They struggled, making noises, above the place where the little bird was flailing, trying to offer it guidance. With their help, the baby bird succeeded in picking up its flight and landing on the branch of a tree.

If we watch a plant grow in slow motion, it is impossible not to feel the miracle of life. No matter how long life means: a day, a year, ten or eighty years. How could you not get emotional when a dog prefers to stay near its puppies instead of leaving them and getting something to eat? And how it drags them back to the shelter to protect them when they begin to explore the world? But the human being is the only one who creates a lifetime relationship with his or her descendants. A relationship where a human life manifests in all its plenitude.

A Parent's Sacrifice

There is a tendency, quite natural for a parent, to sacrifice him or herself for their child. There is nothing more uplifting for the soul in this existence than one person sacrificing for another. But this sacrifice is valuable only if the feelings behind it are clean and orientated toward the other person's good. Yet, it may happen that the sacrifice hides the person's incapability to do other things.

For example, let us say that a mother decides to permanently give up work and stay at home with her child or children. There is absolutely nothing wrong here, neither if she works nor if she stays at home with the baby. But if behind this decision, beyond the desire of taking care of her child, there are other things too, for example, the fear of social failure, the incapacity of finding the right job, comfort, etc., then all these will manifest, sooner or later, in the form of frustration, which will reflect upon the child. Reproaches, irritation, discontent will occur in the relationship between mother and child. All these may happen more on a subconscious level, and this is exactly why we need to become aware of what we feel. We need to find out what is happening in our mind and soul. With wrong motivation we do nothing but deceive ourselves and what we manage to build somewhere it may collapse somewhere else.

The parent's sacrifice is not a currency. I sacrifice for you; instead you will obey to me ever after. The true sacrifice does not follow any personal interest. Sacrifice, as well as helping the other, does not have to create addictions.

There are parents who blackmail their children with what they have done for them. "I did this and that, and you cannot do at least this thing."

Love, respect and listening to the child spring from the love, the respect and the listening (respectively the understanding) of the parent to the child.

Generation Gap

We always hear people talking about the generation gap. Many times, parents and children take this conflict as a given fact, something normal and expected. But nothing can be normal in a conflict, especially between a parent and his or her child. The "generation gap," the conflict between parents and children, does not emerge from nothingness nor simply as a by-product of puberty.

It begins somewhere in childhood and evolves subtly, bursting at the moment when the teenager is preparing to become a grown-up. Its source is in the child's feeling that he is misunderstood and is escalated by his attempts to manifest his individuality. As time passes by, the psychological gap between the child and parent deepens. No matter how different the social context of every generation, people can approach each other by the understanding of human nature in general. If we understand that people are different, if we understand the essence of this diversity, then conflicts can be easily solved.

As a parent it is important to always be close to your child's soul, to have a permanent communication with him, to know his feelings and to understand him. If you do this from the time he is little, the generation gap will never emerge, or in the worst case it will be much diminished. If we did not accept this conflict as something normal, maybe we would do more things to prevent it from emerging. The first step is to understand him. If you do this, everything else will come.

The generation gap, the conflict between parents and children, does not emerge from nothingness nor by a matter of course at puberty.

Generation Connection

When there is a strong connection between generations that is based upon love, respect, and mutual trust, the child easily finds his or her place in the family, but also in the group of friends. There are families lucky enough to include three or four generations: parents, children, and their children all together. When the relationship between the generations works well, it is a great joy to be around them.

A proverb says, "If you want good advice, consult an old man." Unfortunately, this popular wisdom has lost a lot of its power nowadays. We see around us young people's manifestations of contempt and cynicism toward old people. How is thing possible and how can it manifest on such a great scale?

I think that the parents, in the education they give to their children, have neglected moral values, giving priority to other things that seem more important. Unfortunately, the parents themselves have undermined their relationship with their children instead of building confidence and respect, step by step, brick by brick. They have done this by imposing rules the child does not understand, by imposing certain behavior that is contrary to the child's personal instinct. Misunderstood by the person who was supposed to be emotionally the closest to him, the child protects himself by increasing the psychological distance between him and his parent.

The neglect of moral values warrants a price that is paid by the parents—quite expensively.

The psychological distance between parent and child increases as a result of the child being deprived of the most important thing for him: his parent's time and affection. Too many times parents try to compensate for their absence with toys and presents, which represent nothing but a pathetic substitute. Nothing can replace the parent's absence in a child's life.

The psychological distance between the child and his parent is a rupture created in time.

The parents' weaknesses, which the parents themselves ignore, return to them in the form of their child's disrespect. And it is hard to realize what exactly caused it because one or more things may have the same consequence.

Reproach is another factor that affects the trust in the relationship with the child. Reproach is a form of accusation without right of appeal, and it has only negative consequences: the child feels misunderstood, wronged. Therefore, the child's attempt to change something in the given situation will be very small. If you really want to help your child change something, do not use reproaches because you will deepen the state of affairs you want to change.

A positive way of approaching a mistake is talking about it without blaming anybody for it. For example, you may say, "This room is a mess," instead of, "Look what a mess *you* made!" or, "This test contains ten mistakes," instead of, "*You* made ten mistakes." An impersonal approach does not establish somebody's guilt without a prior knowledge and opinion of the person in question. The next step is to see what the *child's opinion* is and try to ascertain his involvement in establishing the measures that could improve the situation.

Another element of the deterioration of the parent-child relationship is the hyper protection of the child. Sometimes parents tend to protect their child in an exaggerated way that leads to the child's addiction to his parents, to his distrust in his own motivations and abilities, and, on the whole, to the weakening of his personality. The child feels his parents' distrust in him, even if he does not express it and even if he is not totally aware of it. This distrust will leave marks both on his personality and on his relationships.

Another great mistake that a parent can make and that directly affects the child's sense of respect is doing everything for the child to make sure everything will be good and comfortable for the child. Although the intention is good, that of helping one's child, the result is fateful. The child is deprived of personal experiences that would help him evolve and at the same time the satisfaction of doing a job himself. Doing the work in the child's place may be easier for the parent than teaching the child how to do it himself. But this will cause him to need props throughout his life instead of living by standing on his own feet.

Your child's confidence in you, no matter if you are twenty, forty, or seventy years old, is the effect of a mutual relationship. The confidence that you gave him as a being capable of taking his life into his own hands, will sooner or later come back to you.

You may ask yourself what connection all these have with young people's respect toward elderly people in general. Well, everything begins from the child's relationship with his parents. You will never see a young person who respects his parents cursing or using bad language in the presence of an elderly person.

Legacy Given Forth

As a parent, the most important thing you do for your child is the education you provide her at home. Nothing has a bigger impact upon your child than the legacy received from her parents. Directly or indirectly, your actions are under the influence of your own parents. When the legacy is healthy, generations of parents will make their presence felt in your child, lighting her path.

If you are in a situation where you would rather bury the received legacy, the simple fact that you are reading this book, or any other book concerning the child's education, proves that you are on the right track, that you want to make a change in the legacy received and you are ready to take action. You are the person who will change things in a positive way for the next generations of children from your family.

**You are the person
who can change the legacy
for the generations to come.**

Every generation passes on a legacy of beliefs and values, enriching it with its own experience. In this flow, every person has a duty that she cannot forget about, the duty to herself. No life should be wasted. The more pleased she is in the relationship with herself, the higher is her capacity to give and to help other people, including her own child.

The human being is the only one who, by her self-conscience, bears the responsibility of her life. As a parent, you have a duty both to your child and to yourself. The concern for you and for her, equally, is a proof of appreciation of your lives.

The help you give to your child is a beautiful legacy from which your child receives the necessary "weapons" to conquer life: love, self-confidence, compassion, freedom to express herself, to name only a few.

Help her discover herself, to form the spirit of a happy life, and to find tranquility within her heart because our inner life is what gives us the strength to do everything we want.

Otopeni, July 8, 2012

Acknowledgments

I want to thank everyone who has had a significant role in my spiritual path and who has left their mark on my heart.

All my gratitude to my parents for the unconditional love they gave me and for all their work throughout their lives.

For my husband, I offer all my gratitude for staying by my side on the long way traveled as one and for all the wonderful things accomplished together, one of them being this book, his contribution to its publishing being significant.

Thank you, Simona. Without your presence in my life this book would have never been written.

I thank Ionela and Codruț for being such wonderful parents, a real source of inspiration for me.

I thank Rodica Indig for existing in my life and for the reference points you offer me all the time.

I thank my friends Octavia and Elisabeta for encouraging me to write this book and for their love.

And last but not least, I thank my friend and editor Gabriela Panaite for her help in the publication of this book.

For the English edition of the book, my special thanks go to the translator Briana Belciug and the copyeditor Bessie Gantt.